ANGLO OVER BRACERO:
A HISTORY OF THE MEXICAN
WORKER IN THE UNITED STATES
FROM ROOSEVELT TO NIXON
PETER N. KIRSTEIN

San Francisco, California

Published By

R AND E RESEARCH ASSOCIATES
4843 Mission Street, San Francisco, 94112
18581 McFarland Avenue, Saratoga, California 95070

Publishers:

Robert D. Reed and Adam S. Eterovich

Library of Congress Card Catalog Number

76-56554

ISBN

0-88247-442-1

INTRODUCTION

The study deals with bracero labor in the United States. This labor provoked antagonistic diplomatic behavior between the United States and Mexico and illustrated how powerful pressure groups could influence and dominate an important aspect of American foreign policy.

My thesis is that American importation of Mexican labor was not necessary to satisfy domestic labor requirements except during the Second World War. Domestic shortages were a product of horrendous working conditions, incredibly low wages and a determined agribusiness conspiracy to keep the native worker off the farm. Big farmers wanted cheap Mexican labor who expected to be treated as an exploited economic commodity and who submitted to arduous work with little compensation.

There were several binational labor agreements which are examined in detail. As with most post-World War II governmental programs, there was a spate of agencies and bureaus involved in the bracero program. The study analyzes the roles of the bureaus and traces their involvement in the raging pressure group controversy between unions which adamantly opposed the importation of alien farm labor and big business interests, who averred that bracero labor was vital to national security.

The bulk of my research was done at the Harry S. Truman Library in Independence, Missouri, and at the National Archives. The highlight of my research was the discovery of a major secret study which uses presently closed Department of State files in an analysis of the major diplomatic disputes between Mexico and the United States arising over the breakdown of the intergovernmental bracero program. Specific Mexican complaints dealt with exploitation, discrimination and indiscriminate hiring of Mexican workers.

The period covered in the study commences with the initial Mexican-American of the mid-nineteenth century. The bulk of the study covers the bracero during the Roosevelt and Truman years, yet traces the bracero crisis up to and including the Nixon Administration.

TABLE OF CONTENTS

CHAPTER I

THE ORIGINAL AMERICANS

Of all the major ethnic minority groups in the United States none have been excluded from the modern industrial economy to the extent of the Mexican Americans. This group has not generally received the same economic, social and political benefits as the majority of Americans. The reason for this state of affairs is at least partially racial, for the Mexican American is at variance racially with white Protestant America. In the vast majority of instances, Mexican Americans are not of pure European lineage. They are an admixture of two to three racial groupings--the Hispanic European, Indian and black.[1] The Indian, of course, was almost exterminated and the black man was enslaved by the predominant white culture. The Mexican American is a product of previously despised races which accounts in part for Mexican American exclusion from, and discrimination against them, by the white society.[2]

The Southwestern part of the United States is where the major interaction between Mexican American and white American has taken place. This region has historically been an agricultural economy which possessed great natural resources, accessibility to ports and a generally congenial climate. The Mexican American for centuries has been a major contributor to the development of this agricultural empire. Significantly, the Mexican national provided the labor which led to an economic empire--he was a "charter member minority".[3] Mexicans lived in the Southwest when it was part of Mexico, before it became United States territory. The Texas Rebellion of 1836, which was a major precipitator of the Mexican-United States War, ended with an independent Texas only later to be annexed to the United States in 1845. As a result of the war, Mexico lost 918,355 square miles of land --more than one-half of its pre-war territory. Present-day California, Utah, Nevada and large sections of New Mexico, Arizona, Colorado and Wyoming were included in the former Mexican territory which was ceded to the United States in the Treaty of Guadelupe Hidalgo. This treaty was ratified by the Senate on May 30, 1848.[4]

Present-day Mexican Americans who are descendants of those who lived in the Southwest before the United States acquired it are part of this charter member minority group. These descendants primarily reside in northern New Mexico and southern Colorado.[5] However, this notion of historic primacy permeates the entire Mexican American population which includes both the original descendants and descendants of Mexicans who migrated to the United States after 1848.[6] Unlike European immigrants, who, although not being primary settlers were generally assimilated into the social and economic culture, the Mexican American, despite his charter member status, did not reap the gains afforded to the dominant alien culture. This perennial minority status appears more tragic and unjustifiable when one sees the immense economic contributions this ethnic minority has given to the Southwest and other areas as well.

The Mexican American, in spite of his inferior status, contributed to the economic and cultural development of the southwestern United States from the Treaty of Guadelupe Hidalgo to 1900. This period is characterized by many historical trends which still continue.

Shortly after the Mexican-United States War, the Gold Rush exploded upon the scene in California and other Western States. Spanish-speaking Americans, besides enriching themselves, contributed technological assistance to the throng of gold-seeking, English-speaking Americans.[7] Americans were unfamiliar with placer and bonanza mining, they had no mining law, "so they adopted the ancient Spanish law under which the right of property depends upon the discovery and development of the mine."[8] Tools to extract the mineral were of Spanish origin such as the batea, a flat-bottomed pan.[9]

Despite the obvious importance of the Mexican American during the Gold Rush, they endured treatment that was similar, although less severe, to that accorded other native minority groups who occupied lands that lay in the way of onrushing Anglo-Americans. Thousands of "forty-niners" dispossessed those Mexicans who inhabited the gold fields. In the early 1850s, Mexicans were expelled from the Sierra Nevada mines.[10] After they were driven from the gold fields they were relegated to an inferior economic status on land now owned by the Anglos.[11]

Anglo hostility and mistreatment of the Mexican was not confined to economic persecution, for there developed a general anti-Mexican climate of violence throughout the Borderlands with Mexico. Lynchings acquired a semi-official status in Texas with the legendary Texas Rangers directing organized violence against Mexican Americans.[12] This white-initiated violence was justified for two reasons: whites believed Mexicans were helping runaway slaves, and Mexicans were envied and resented because they could transport freight from inland cities to the coast by oxen cheaper than could white Texans. In retaliation, masked bands of men murdered Mexican cart drivers and destroyed their cargoes.[13] These activities triggered a Mexican Government complaint to Washington which led to a State Department investigation in 1856.[14]

The displacement of the Mexican from his land and his submission to violence by the Anglos subjected the Mexican to an inferior social status unlike his previous position of social dominance.[15] White westward migration which was economically motivated, created a new social order where landless Mexicans became strangers in their own land. Since most did not own land, those who felt the greatest impact of the new order were those who lost the most--the landed Mexican middle class: "The bulk of the Mexican American population simply noted the exchange of one oppressive regime (the landed Spanish) for another and went on working and living as they had before."[16] Since most Mexican Americans were accustomed to a minority status, they did not resent the change in land ownership from elite Mexican to Anglos. They were still slaves--only the master had changed his color.

With the Anglos came the railroad, which enabled the cattle, sheep, cotton, lettuce, produce, wool and beef industries to prosper in the southwest. The railroad also provided the means for conveying the goods to larger consumer markets. In the 1880s, the railroads utilized Mexican labor on construction crews, maintenance crews and as section hands.[17] The Southern Pacific and Santa Fe Railroads employed bracero labor in the 1880s in extending their lines through the desert regions of the Southwest.[18] The modern phase of southwestern United States development dates from the arrival of the railroad, which was constructed and maintained to a significant extent by Mexican labor.

The railroad also assumes transcendant importance because it marked the initial attempt at importing Mexican national labor to assist in the development of the United States' economy.

> The principal large-scale importers of Mexican labor...the railroads kept recruiting additional workers in Mexico. ...Recruited by labor agents...Mexicans were assembled in El Paso and from there sent out on six-month work contracts with the Southern Pacific and Santa Fe. ... Starting around 1900, railroad recruitment reached its peak in 1910 and 1912. ...Mexicans were used after 1905 in an ever-widening arc which gradually extended through Colorado, Wyoming, Utah, Montana, Idaho, Oregon and Washington.[19]

This initial Mexican importation was without international control because the contracts were on a worker-to-employer basis. There were no agreements between the United States and Mexico, between the railroads and the United States, or between the railroads and Mexico to guarantee working conditions of Mexican national labor. The magnitude of this importation is dramatically shown by Carey McWilliams, an historian and activist for Mexican American rights who has written extensively on the history of the Mexican American, when he cites a Labor Department investigation which concluded that most Mexicans living in the United States in 1912 had at one time been an employee for the railroads.[20]

Mexicans were also important in the early twentieth-century development of the cotton industry in the southwest. The majority of these Mexican nationals provided an impetus for cotton's replacement of cattle as the major industry in Texas and Oklahoma.[21] By the 1930s, they were cultivating millions of acres of cotton in these two states.[22] The Texas farmer, who generations earlier committed violence against Mexicans whom he perceived as a potential economic threat, now rejoiced at the presence of the Mexican: "We cannot do without Mexicans here. ...they work cheaper and are willing as tenants to pay higher rents or more of the crops."[23]

The period from the end of the Mexican-United States War in 1848 to 1930 was a formative period in the history of the Mexican in the United States. This period witnessed numerous episodes of racial, social and economic violence directed against this ethnic minority group. Lynchings, normally thought to have been reserved for blacks only, were used against Mexicans in the post-Civil War period. In addition, Mexicans as well as freed slaves were unable to own land. The former had their land confiscated while the latter were denied an unfulfilled promise. The presence of contemporary Chicano political and racial consciousness can trace much of its frustration and anger to this period.

Other salient features of this period were the pivotal contributions of the Mexican American and the Mexican national to the southwest's burgeoning economy and the beginnings of large-scale labor importation from Mexico. Both native and imported Mexican labor contributed enormously to the growth of the region: they planted cotton and sugar beets, and maintained the railroad. This "stoop" labor provided a major ingredient in the development of the modern agribusiness industry which requires an enormously large cheap labor supply. To insure this steady available supply of labor, Mexicans were imported into the United States. Employers efficiently operated this importation by paying Mexican contractors to truck Mexicans into the United States.[24] Indeed, its efficiency is borne out by the fact that the present Mexican American population has evolved, to a great extent, from the Mexican national immigrants who were imported from Mexico in the late nineteenth and early twentieth centuries.

There has been an acceleration and intensification of existing nineteenth-century trends during the twentieth century. The more prominent ones have been the climactic development of large-scale productive farming (agribusiness) which reached its takeoff point in terms of productivity and numbers of employees.

The tidal wave of Mexican immigration erupted in the early twentieth century. A major, yet statistically uncertain, component of this immigration is the wetback; wetbacks are Mexicans who swim across the Rio Grande River in order to enter the United States as illegal immigrants. Although many Mexican enter overland by illegally crossing wire fences (so-called alambristas), the term "wetback" is applied to all Mexican nationals who enter illegally or surreptitiously into the United States. Another major element of this twentieth-century Mexican exodus are Mexicans directly recruited by Americans. Beginning in 1942, Mexican imported labor was brought in under international contract; before that, it was indiscriminately recruited by agribusiness and railroad interests. A third major component is Mexicans who seek permanent residence in the United States.

The domestic situation in Mexico as well as domestic demands in the United States contributed to the forces behind the emigration. Mexico in the early twentieth century was racked by violent revolution. The overthrow of the Porfirio Diaz regime in 1911, with its attendant social dislocations, served as a major "push force" for a massive Mexican migration to the United States.[25] In the previous decade, 1900-1910, only 24,000 Mexicans entered legally into the United States; from 1910-1920, approximately 250,000 Mexicans arrived.[26] These war refugees entered a dynamic economic situation in the United States which, combined with the domestic crisis in Mexico, provided an environment for continuous immigration into the United States.

After 1915, United States' preparations for the First World War acted as a major "pull" force complementing the "push" forces of the Mexican Revolution. The allied demand for American products accelerated with the outbreak of the First World War; American farmers were attracted to the cities by the lure of industrial employment. In addition, native farm manpower was being drained by the armed forces. Chinese immigration, which had been eliminated since the nineteenth century and the Gentleman's Agreement of 1907, which curtailed Japanese immigration also contributed to the lack of an adequate farm labor supply.[27]

Mexico began to complain of the deleterious domestic effects of this emigration in the first few decades of the twentieth century. Generally, these complaints centered on the depopulation and industrial and agricultural retardation. The Liberal Party, an opposition party to Diaz, declared in 1906 that "spoilation and tyranny" had caused "the depopulation of Mexico as thousands of our fellow countrymen have had to cross the border in flight."[28]

From 1900-1925, Mexican imported nationals began to penetrate the entire United States. There is conclusive knowledge that Mexicans did not reside solely in the southwest and although they were less assimilable than western Europeans, some did adapt to an urban industrial culture. Beginning in 1916, they began appearing in small numbers as workers in the steel mills and packaging plants in Chicago and Gary, Indiana.[29] In the 1920s, they worked for United States Steel in Ohio and Bethlehem Steel in Pennsylvania; by the 1930s, there were over 20,000 Mexicans in Chicago alone.[30]

It is significant, however, that there were no inroads into skilled industrial or clerical positions. Permanent Mexican urban colonies did not develop. This lack of a large Mexican urban population is in direct contrast to European immigrant groups who lived in urban areas adjacent to the industries in which they were employed. The European migrant initially lived in a major urban metropolitan area where he acquired political influence and was befriended by the city boss. The result was social mobility in which many became civil servants or entered the clerical professions. The Mexican minority did not attain these white collar positions because they were literally kept down on the farm. Southwestern agribusiness interests were opposed to the siphoning off of their labor supply to northern and eastern industrial interests and feared should Mexican labor displace white native labor by depressing the prevailing wage rate, this in turn would produce northern nativist attempts at quota restrictions which in turn would eliminate the source of Mexican national migratory rural farm labor.[31]

Another reason for the absence of permanent Mexican penetration into industrial areas throughout the United States, was the existence of an informal Mexican quota immigration policy. Largely for diplomatic reasons, the Federal Government in March, 1929, adopted a policy of "administration restriction" by informally tightening up the enforcement of existing immigration restrictions with the cooperation of the Mexican Government. There was an unsuccessful attempt to pass a bill in 1926, which would have applied the quota provisions of the Immigration Act of 1924 (Johnson-Reed Act) to Mexicans.[32] These events-- agribusiness' fear of losing its labor supply to northern and eastern industrial interests and the rising occurrence of nativism in the 1920s--prevented any widespread Mexican entrance into urban employment.

In the 1930s there was not only an end to Mexican penetration of the urban economic sector but also a widespread deportation of Mexicans. The result was outmigration which created grave and dramatic repercussions in the Mexican National and Mexican American communities in the United States during the depression. Many states, from Minnesota to California, used various means of eliminating "surplus" Mexican labor from their relief rolls.[33]

In Denver, the Bureau of Public Welfare attempted to retard the rural-to-urban migration of destitute Mexican sugar beet workers. The Bureau sent letters to sugar beet workers throughout the State imploring them to stay on the fields and "advised them of the critical relief situation and of the necessity of conserving earnings.[34] Many state repatriation programs indiscriminately returned many thousands of Mexican nationals and Mexican Americans to Mexico in order to ease the load of welfare agencies and to eliminate Mexican competition for jobs. Pressure and harassment were not infrequently used as methods of persuasion.[35]

Many standard accounts of Mexican repatriations in the 1930s stress the United States' role with little mention of Mexican encouragement or participation in repatriating 100,000 Mexicans.[36] Only the United States is blamed for the excesses of this outmigration in which only 27,000 Mexicans entered the United States during the 1930s and in which there was a decline of Mexican-born Americans from 639,000 in 1930 to 377,000 in 1940.[37]

Although many Mexicans were repatriated by federal and private local welfare agencies attempting to diminish their relief rolls and others were repatriated through federal raids conducted by the United States Border Patrol, many returned through their own volition or were returned with the assistance and encouragement of the Mexican Government.

Examples are numerous of United States-sponsored and initiated repatriation episodes. In the early 1930s, Mexicans were returned to Mexico from Michigan, northern Illinois and Minnesota with United States public relief funds. In 1932, Mexican nationals were repatriated from Michigan at the number of 1500. Thousands more were repatriated during the winter of 1933, at a cost estimated between $75,000 to $100,000.[38] In a single day in November, 1932, one hundred repatriates left St. Paul, Minnesota, at the expense of the Bureau of Public Welfare. Although financed through United States agencies, the repatriation was voluntary--they were not deported. The Council of Social Agencies of Chicago which handled repatriations from that city would not expel a Mexican "without first weighing the depth of the client's stake in the United States. ...The social worker must consider with unusual care questions relating to deportability."[39]

In March, 1934, 300 Mexicans were repatriated from Ohio, a state where Mexicans worked in steel mills. Ohio in this instance paid the requisite train fare to Mexico. The Civil Works Administration, a New Deal work relief agency created in 1933, sponsored deportation directed by the State Civil Works Administration Director, E. O. Braught.[40] There are, however, major exceptions to United States-initiated repatriation episodes which lessen the stigma attributed to the United States.

It is possible to conjecture, if not verify, that many Mexicans returned to Mexico in the 1930s because of the perceived economic inducements in Mexico. Contrary to the chaotic days of the revolution against Diaz and the ensuing civil wars, Mexico was engineering expensive public works programs, reorganizing the school system and creating a "generous homesteading plan that suddenly made the homeland more attractive than the states."[41] Given the depression-devastated economic order in the United States, the Mexican certainly could have adopted a nostalgic feeling for home. The barest possibility of economic improvement in Mexico could have created the context of the 1930s, a powerful outmigration impluse--the feeling that this time life would be better in Mexico than in the United States.

Mexico, which had been previously critical of the economic consequences of the Mexican national emigration, was directly involved in repatriation episodes. In Austin, Texas, during April, 1934, Rafael de La Colima, Mexican Consul General, implemented attempts to repatriate 618 Mexicans. In addition, Mexican families of both United States and Mexican citizenship who expressed a desire to continue residing in the United States were allowed to do so.[42]

Another seldom emphasized fact was the desire of the highest Mexican Government officials to have their citizens returned to Mexico. Lazaro Cárdenas, leftist Nationalist President of Mexico from 1934-1940, who expropriated British and United States oil interests in March, 1938, agonized over the problems of Mexicans residing in the United States in the 1930s.

By February, 1937, there were approximately 2,500,000 Mexicans in the United States, of which eighty per cent or 2,000,000 were unemployed.[43] Cárdenas in the early months of 1937, initiated several discussions with prominent Mexican Americans to arrange for Mexican financial assistance for jobless Mexicans.[44] The problems of insufficient relief for Mexican nations was intensified by the indiscriminate removal of many Mexican Americans from the relief rolls. This created an atmosphere in which Mexican Americans were afraid to apply for relief, in which, "it takes only an insinuation from an official in the United States to create widespread fear among the Mexican immigrants of deportation if they apply for relief."[45] There emerged a Mexican Government dilemma for it was too poor to finance adequately the repatriation of all its citizens and too poor to offer sufficient welfare relief for those stranded in the United States. The dilemma reached its climax in 1938. *Millions w/o a country*

President Cárdenas undertook to build agrarian colonies which would work the recently expropriated oil fields. The intention was to return thousands of Mexicans living in Texas, California and other southwestern states. The Eighteenth of March Colony established near Brownsville, Texas, was the first of these colonies established. By 1939, 500 Mexicans were living there.[46]

In July, 1939, Cárdenas directed his American-educated Undersecretary of State, Ramon Beteta, to arrange for the repatriation of 1,400,000 additional Mexicans. Beteta held mass rallies in Los Angeles and San Francisco to recruit for farm colonies in Chihuahua and Lower California. In these colonies the government planned to grant every repatriated farmer twenty-five acres and a loan to purchase seed, tools and supplies.[47] Cárdenas, who was obsessed with the independent non-colonial development of the Mexican economy, hoped that the repatriation of United States-trained Mexican farmers would stimulate the agricultural economy. Without adequate capital, the Cárdenas repatriation dreams were doomed to failure.

Ignacio Garcia Tellez, Mexican Minister of the Interior, announced that his Department, which was heavily involved in repatriation, was forced to forego this endeavor because of insufficient funds.[48] Mexico, in spite of some previously mentioned economic reforms was experiencing enormous economic problems in the 1930s from both the world depression and lingering post-revolutionary dislocations. The intent of the above is not to deny that many Mexicans, either United States citizens or Mexican nationals, were treated harshly by United States welfare agencies or to deny that many were illegally deported. Mexican Americans and nationals were considered racially inferior to whites and not entitled to receive dwindling welfare benefits. Given the economic consequences of the depression in the United States and the reluctant abdication of Mexico to care for its nationals, it appears inevitable, however, that Mexicans in the United States were to suffer greatly. They were simply without any governmental protection. These Mexicans were nationals in name only, in that their financially bankrupt mother country was incapable of assistance and their newly adopted country was experiencing its own financial chaos and deliberately neglecting its responsibilities to non-citizens working in the United States. The repatriation of established Mexican Americans, however, can only be attributed to racism and indifference toward native minority group suffering.

This period from 1900-1940 was a turbulent period for Mexican nationals and citizens in the United States. The Southwest underwent enormous economic growth, so that by 1930 forty per cent of the nation's vegetables, fruit and truck crops were produced in this area.[49] This extraordinary development would have been impossible without the use of Mexican labor, which accounted for sixty per cent of the common labor in Southwestern mines and sixty-five to eight-five percent of the work force on eighteen western railroads.[50]

Except for the 1930s, Mexican mass migration to the United States was a salient characteristic of this period. This migration was generally one of drift without stringent government quota systems of enforcement. Initially, the migration was pushed by Mexican political turbulence and later pulled by United States commercial agriculture. It was not until the 1940s that Mexican migration to the United States became subject to government regulation and supervision.

The first four decades of the twentieth century was the period during which the California farmer and Mexican farm laborer established their modern relationship.[51] Because of the Mexican's willingness to labor amid heat, aridity and dust and the demise of Oriental immigration, the former ascended to a position as the primary source of field labor.[52] They became indispensible in the eyes of Southwestern commercial agriculturalists.

Mexican diplomatic involvement and concern over the living conditions of its nationals increased during the 1900-1940 period. Mexico, which was later to become intensely involved during the 1940s in the whole area of Mexican life in the United States, can trace its origins of concern to the protestations of the 1850s, the Liberal Party pronouncement of 1906, and the active, if unresolved, concern of the Cárdenas years of the 1930s.

The 1940s and 1950s are decades when the importation of the Mexican becomes an institutionalized fact of life. Various Mexican-United States agreements are consummated throughout the period and there is continuous governmental preoccupation with these importation programs. Many of the pre-1940 trends of diplomatic tension, Mexican importation, racial discrimination and permanent minority status reach climactic heights in the 1940s and early 1950s and eventually cause the ruin of the intergovernmental labor program.

Footnotes:

1. Manuel P. Servin, The Mexican Americans: An Awakening Majority (Beverly Hills: Glencoe Press, 1970), p. 1.

2. Ibid.

3. Everett C. Hughes and Helen MacGill Hughes, Where People Meet: Racial and Ethnic Frontiers (New York: The Free Press, 1952), p. 23

4. Henry Steel Commager, ed., Documents of American History (7th edition; New York: Appleton-Century-Crofts, 1967), pp. 313-14.

5. Leo Grebler, Joan W. Moore and Ralph C. Guzman, The Mexican American People: The Nation's Second Largest Minority (New York: The Free Press, 1970), p. 46.

6. Ibid.

7. Ruth S. Lamb, Mexican Americans: Sons of the Southwest (Claremont: Ocelot Press, 1970), p. 99.

8. Ibid., p. 100.

9. Ibid.

10. Ibid.

11. Julian Nava, Mexican Americans: A Brief Look at Their History (New York: Anti-Defamation League of B'Nai B'rith, 1970), p. 28.

12. Lamb, Sons of Southwest, p. 101. Discrimination in Texas became a major issue during the wartime Mexican bracero program.

13. J. F. Rippy, "Border Troubles Along the Rio Grande", Southwestern Historical Quarterly, 23 (October 1919), 98.

14. Ibid.

15. Wayne Moquin, A Documentary History of the Mexican American (New York: Praeger, 1971), p. 190.

16. Ibid., p. 191.

17. Carey McWilliams, North From Mexico (New York: Greenwood Press, 1968), p. 167. Mexican nationals helped maintain United States railroads from 1943-1945 as part of the wartime labor agreement between Mexico and the United States.

18. Ibid. Bracero is a Spanish term which refers to a rural farm hand. It refers to one who works with his arms. The Spanish word for arm is brazo.

19. Ibid., pp. 168-69.

20. Ibid., p. 168.

21. Ibid., p. 170.

22. Remsen Crawford, "The Menance of Mexican Immigration", Current History, 31 (February 1930), 904.

23. Ibid., p. 906.

24. McWilliams, North, p. 168.

25. Lamb, Sons of Southwest, p. 105.

26. Ernesto Galarza, Merchants of Labor: The Mexican Bracero Story (Charlotte: McNally and Loftin, 1964), p. 28.

27. Lamb, Sons of Southwest, p. 106.

28. Galarza, Merchants, p. 28.

29. McWilliams, North, p. 184.

30. Ibid.

31. Ibid., pp. 184-85.

32. Ibid., p. 185.

33. Nava, A Brief Look, p. 34.

34. The Survey, March, 1937, p. 82.

35. Nava, A Brief Look, p. 34.

36. Some of the standard accounts include Emory S. Bogardus, The Mexican in the United States (Los Angeles: University of Southern California Press, 1934): Ruth S. Lamb, Mexican Americans: Sons of the Southwest, previously cited. See also Carey McWilliams, "Getting Rid of the Mexican Americans", American Mercury, 27 (March 1933).

37. Grebler et al., pp. 66, 526.

38. The Survey, January, 1933, 69.

39. Ibid.

40. New York Times, March 20, 1934. (Hereafter NYT).

41. NYT, March 30, 1937.

42. NYT, April 1, 1934. However, within four months, Mexican Americans in Austin were denied the right to vote due to their not belonging to the white race. Perhaps such discrimination was based on repatriation aims as well as racist intentions. See NYT, July 27, 1934.

43. NYT, February 18, 1937.

44. Ibid.

45. Bogardus, The Mexican, p. 95; cited in Grebler et al.

46. Newsweek, July 31, 1939, p. 11.

47. Ibid.

48. NYT, January 23, 1938.

49. McWilliams, North, p. 185.

50. Ibid., pp. 185-186.

51. Galarza, Merchants, p. 32.

52. Ibid., p. 14.

CHAPTER II

THE FARM SECURITY ADMINISTRATION AND THE BRACERO

The Second World War precipitated another mass migration of Mexican workers to the United States. The fear of an insufficient population to wage a foreign war and provide domestic goods and services provided an American rationale for seeking alien labor in the late 1930s and early 1940s. A New York Times editorial reflected the fear of a massive labor shortage.

> Indications grow that the U.S....will find its most serious problem in the total labor supply. Shortages are already serious enough in skilled labor, but a shortage of labor as a whole appears by no means remote. In order to meet it successfully, a far-flung mobilization of labor resources seems certain to be necessary.[1]

A Bureau of Agricultural Economics report prepared for the Department of Agriculture in October, 1939, estimated that 1,695,000 farmers would leave for the cities.[2] There were various reasons for this reduction in the farm population. The presidential signing of the Selective Service and Training Act in September, 1940, had important effects on the labor supply. Manpower requirements for the armed services reduced the farm population by 280,000 from April 1, 1940, to January 1, 1942.[3] Under the initial act, agricultural workers could be exempted only if they were engaged in commercial farming and could prove their indispensable importance to the maintenance of the farm enterprise. As farm labor continued to dwindle, Secretary of Agriculture Claude R. Wickard began to exert pressure on Selective Service officials to dictate more liberal agricultural deferment procedures to the local boards.[4] Wickard emphasized that farm labor had decreased 17.8% between April, 1940, and April, 1941; Wickard succeeded by the end of 1941 in persuading Selective Service officials to treat farm labor in certain agricultural areas as a national defense requirement.[5] Brigadier General Lewis B. Hershey, director of the Selective Service System, told the American Bar Association in September, 1941, that he was alarmed "over the fact that in a short period over 1,000,000 agricultural workers have left the farms for the cities and the industrial areas."[6]

Another major cause for the reduction of the farm labor sector was the allurement of jobs in the defense industry. Defense industry offered attractive alternatives to irregular hours and unpredictable income earnings. Indeed, this desire for high wages and regular hours swept many thousands from the farm to the defense plant. Significantly, the jobs were there. Secretary of Labor Frances Perkins dramatically indicated the need for additional workers in the defense industries in June, 1941, when she predicted a shortage of 1,408,600 defense industry workers.

...323,900 additional workers will be needed by the shipbuilding industry, 408,400 by aircraft, 291,600 by machine tools and ordnance and 384,700 by other defense industries. ...It is estimated ...227,500 unskilled workers will be needed.[7]

Farm worker migration to defense industries had profound results on the agricultural scene in California. In the late 1930s and early 1940s migration reached its peak with Okies arriving by the thousands.[8] In spite of this enormous out-of-state influx, there emerged serious farm labor deficiencies. Most of the Okies and much of the native California farm population were attracted to defense jobs and regardless "of the record breaking migration, there was a shortage of farm labor."[9]

This farm labor shortage triggered demands throughout the West and Southwest for the importation of Mexican labor. In July, 1941, Arizona cotton growers requested the removal of importation restrictions.[10] Agricultural groups in Texas and New Mexico in September, 1941, sent a signed petition to the Immigration and Naturalization Service requesting permission to import 30,000 Mexican farm workers. The Southern Pacific also petitioned the Immigration and Naturalization Service to allow Mexican workers to assist in railroad maintenance.[11] The government denied these initial requests, asserting it wished to avoid needless alien importation and its policy was that job vacancies be filled first by United States citizens. The government felt it would be politically hazardous to import foreigners to do work that might displace available domestic labor. In 1941, the government took the position of analyzing separately each individual request for Mexican labor. This was accomplished with the United States Employment Service entering the area in question and assessing the particular labor shortage situation. If a labor shortage existed, the USES would initially recruit domestic labor. Depending on whether there existed a domestic labor shortage or whether domestic labor was available, the USES would deliver its recommendation for or against alien importation to the Immigration and Naturalization Service.[12]

After the Japanese attack on Pearl Harbor which triggered the United States' entry into the Second World War in December, 1941, the government did an about-face with regard to its previous intransigence in hiring Mexican labor. The sudden entrance into the war convinced many officials that a labor shortage was an acute problem. The USES, which refused to comply with requests in 1941 for alien labor, suddenly changed its position in 1942. It recommended to the Immigration and Naturalization Service on May 12, 1942, that 3,000 Mexicans be used to augment the sugar beet labor force in California.[13]

In the spring of 1942, an interagency farm labor group was created to investigate intensively the total farm labor population problem and develop contingency plans for alien importation.[14] The agencies that comprised the group were the War Manpower Commission, the Department of Agriculture, the Department of State, the Department of Labor, the Department of Justice and the Office of the Coordinator of Inter-American Affairs.[15] In devising a plan for Mexican labor importation it became immediately apparent that any scheme would require Mexican approval. In June, 1942, an official request for Mexican labor was made to the Mexican Government and on July 13, 1942, meetings between the United States and Mexico began in Mexico City. The United States delegation consisted of two officials from the Department of Agriculture and an embassy staff member. These were John O. Walker, Assistant Administrator of the Farm Security Administration, David Meeker, Assistant Director of the Office of Agricultural War Relations, and J. F. McGurk, Counselor of the American Embassy in Mexico. The Mexican delegation consisted of E. Hidalgo acting as representative of the Foreign Office and Abraham J. Navas, representative of the Department of Labor and Social Provision.[16]

Before any United States-Mexican agreement could be finalized, it was necessary to overcome various Mexican objections. Mexico had always been critical of United States' racial prejudice and discrimination against Mexican nationals. Furthermore, many Mexicans who were not repatriated in the 1930s floundered in the United States because neither government could or would support them. Consequently, the Mexican Government indicated to Secretary Wickard in June, 1942, that emigration was undesirable "because of previous experiences the (Mexican) government had had with large numbers of Mexican workers who had been stranded in the United States."[17]

The Mexican Government had passed legislation to insure the well-being of any Mexican workers that another nation contracted. During the Great Depression, Mexico paid the return transportation costs for many repatriated Mexicans. Article 123 of the Mexican Constitution stipulates that return transportation must be borne by the employer nation.[18] Article 29 of the Mexican Labor Law of 1931 reiterated that return transportation be provided; it guaranteed that Mexican workers receive a minimum wage and declared that all guarantees be written into each individual worker contract, which must be approved by the Mexican Government.[19] When the United States met with Mexico to determine the provisions for a United States-Mexican agreement, it was negotiating with a nation that was sensitive to previous abuses and had since incorporated legislation to deal with them. For a final agreement to be consummated, it would have to defer to Mexican migratory labor legislation; the War Manpower Commission and the Department of Agriculture were the agencies which sponsored the agreement and can be credited for creating a satisfactory document.

The first Mexican-United States agreement was signed on July 23, 1942, by representatives of both countries and became operationalized with an exchange of notes between George S. Messersmith, United States Ambassador to Mexico, and Ezequial Padilla, Minister for Foreign Affairs in Mexico City, on August 4, 1942. Messersmith in his note to Padilla acknowledged that Mexico was sacrificing labor was was "indispensable" to Mexican agricultural production for the "Continental Defense Program". The thrust of Messersmith's message was an expression of gratitude for Mexican labor which would enable the United States to wage the war against the common enemy.[20] Padilla's message strongly noted the temporary nature of the farm labor program and his country's need for farm labor:

> This department considers itself under the obligation, first of all, of pointing out the importance for the country at the present moment of conserving intact its human material...in which... the intensification of activities and especially agricultural production take <u>first rank</u>.[21]

Having affirmed the primacy of Mexican labor for Mexico, Padilla then took cognizance of the temporary nature of Mexican worker emigration. Finally, Padilla reaffirmed the agreement stipulation that Mexican workers could only perform essential work under conditions enumerated in the agreement.[22]

President Franklin D. Roosevelt stressed the military nature of the bracero program as providing strategic farm crops for the democratic cause in the Second World War. Roosevelt described the August, 1942, agreement as "eloquent witness" to the important role Mexico was playing in the "war of (food) production, upon which the inevitable success of our military program depends."[23]

The agreement incorporated many Mexican demands and generally attempted to guarantee nondiscriminatory treatment for Mexicans.[24] Mexicans were exempted from United States military service. Significantly, this was the first of four "General Provisions" underscoring the military necessity of importing non-military farm workers. In the second, Mexicans were guaranteed nondiscriminatory treatment as enunciated in Roosevelt's Executive Order 8802. This order, which created the Committee on Fair Employment Practice, pertained only to fair treatment in defense industries and government employment; it ignored fair employment practices in agriculture or non-governmental operations.[25] The third general provision mentioned directly Article 29 of the Mexican Labor Law pertaining to transportation, living expenses and repatriation. This provision illustrated United States acknowledgement of Mexico's right to determine binational labor policy and represented the change from a unilateral to a bilateral foreign farm labor program.

Between the wars, Mexicans were imported directly by private American economic interests without any governmental guarantees. There were no attempts to placate Mexican fears of depopulation, for this unilateral American initiated importation program complemented the imperialist Latin American foreign policy of Woodrow Wilson, Warren Harding, Calvin Coolidge and Herbert Hoover. The so-called Good Neighbor Policy of Roosevelt, while still accepting the ultimate goal of American political-economic hegemony in Latin America, officially acknowledged Latin American sovereignty and repudiated the right of military intervention. The fourth general provision declared that Mexican labor would be employed only in places where a labor shortage was certified and could not be competitively hired in order to depress wages domestic workers were receiving.

Contracts had to be printed in both Spanish and English with each Mexican receiving his own copy. The agreement cited Mexican Statute Law as directing that round trip transportation be paid by the United States.

The agreement did not specify the number of Mexicans who could emigrate but allowed for the United States to periodically request the number desired with the Mexican Government making the ultimate decision. No terminal date was included in the agreement but the pact provided for "either government (to give) appropriate notification to the other Government 90 days in advance."

The nexus of the agreement dealt with wages and employment. The essence of the eleven provisions dealing with wages and employment was the assurance of equal treatment. It guaranteed Mexicans an hourly wage of thirty cents, thereby accepting the minimum wage provision of Article 29. This wage rate could be increased if domestic labor received a higher wage for the same work in the same region. This provision reiterated the principle of the fourth "General Provision" which prevented American employers from hiring alien labor to displace or lower the wages of domestic labor. Mexicans could perform only agricultural tasks unless the worker or his government decided otherwise. Mexican nationals received guarantees of housing conditions and sanitary and medical services equal to those of United States labor. Mexicans were guaranteed employment up to 75% of their stay in the United States; if an able worker was prevented from working 75% of the time, he was entitled to receive a daily subsistence allowance of $3.00 for each day unemployed. Even if the alien were working less than 75% of the period, he was still guaranteed subsistence "on the same bases (as) for farm laborers in the United States." Although the length of the individual contracts was not stipulated within the international agreement, workers were compelled to return to Mexico when their contracts expired unless the worker was physically unable to repatriate himself.

There was a provision for a savings fund in which 10% of the farm workers' income would be returned to Mexico and later used to purchase United States agricultural implements.[26]

The August, 1942, international agreement declared that the Farm Security Administration of the Department of Agriculture would be the principal government agency in handling the foreign labor importation program. The Farm Security Administration was in control of the officially designated Mexican Farm Labor Transportation Program from August, 1942, to the end of April, 1943.[27] A total of 15,199 Mexican workers were contracted during this period. From August to December, 1942, 4,152 Mexicans were imported and 11,047 Mexican workers arrived in the United States between January and April, 1943, with the majority going to California, Washington and Arizona.[28] The actual operation of the Mexican Farm Labor Transportation Program began when 500 workers arrived in Stockton, California, on September 30, 1942.[29]

Before workers could be admitted to the United States, their need had to be certified through an elaborate process. Farmers must initially attempt to allay the labor shortage by hiring available domestic labor; the "Fourth General Provision", it should be recalled, emphasized that "Mexicans...should not be employed to displace other workers."[30] Should the farmer be faced with an inadequate domestic labor supply the next step was to seek help from the regional USES office, which would attempt to locate domestic labor.[31] Should domestic labor be available but at a distance, the Farm Security Administration would transport it, charging the farmer for the first 200 miles of transportation. If the USES were unable to locate any available American labor, it would certify to the Farm Security Administration that a domestic labor shortage existed. An order from Attorney General Francis Biddle on September 14, 1942, slightly changed this procedure by authorizing the Immigration and Naturalization Service instead of the Farm Security Administration to grant temporary admission to Mexican agricultural workers after the USES had certified the need.[32] Once admitted, they were to be utilized in areas "where such labor is customarily employed, such as the cotton areas of the Southwest and sugar beet areas of the West."[33]

Throughout its existence from 1937 to 1946, the Farm Security Administration was always under attack. Because of its passionate concern in implementing government protection for minority groups and poor farmers, it was violently besieged by conservative farm organizations such as the American Farm Bureau Federation, backed by 150 county farm bureaus. While conservative groups resented its philosophy of governmental activism and its concern for those farm groups which were alienated from public concern, the Farm Security Administration "commanded (the) highest esteem among liberals in and out of agriculture."[34] The tumultous existence of the Farm Security Administration included its operation of the Mexican Farm Labor Transportation Program.

Is. A Return to Laissez Faire?

The FSA attempted to secure minimum living standards and employment legislation for domestic farm labor. Although the international agreement guaranteed these for Mexican labor in the United States, comparable guarantees were not provided for United States farm workers. Officials of the Farm Security Administration thought it incongrous that a bilateral international agreement would provide welfare legislation for citizens of only one of those countries. Conversely, many agribusiness farmers feared unbridled government regulation and socialization of American agriculture.[35] What the growers desired was decentralization of the now government-operated foreign labor program and a return to grower recruitment of Mexican labor. The growers' primary concern was crops; the FSA was concerned about those who worked the crops.[36]

The popularity of the FSA was not enhanced by Mexico's termination of the Mexican farm labor program on February 8, 1943. Growers charged the FSA was in part responsible for the abrogation because it was too rigid in demanding compliance from United States farmers and misrepresented to Mexico the farmers' attitude to the bracero program. Throughout the 1940s, Mexico frequently terminated or threatened to terminate its contribution of Mexican labor to the United States. It is important to recall that Mexico, historically, had been opposed to discrimination in the United States and concerned about the effects stemming from the loss of young vigorous workers to the North. This initial Mexican termination of the alien farm labor program was created by many factors: internal political difficulties; growing displeasure with United States farmers' compliance with the program; internal pressure to keep the workers home; and dissatisfaction with the enforcement of protective guarantees for Mexican workers. After intense efforts by the United States to placate Mexican demands, Mexico resumed recruitment on March 16, 1943.[37] This latter agreement contained several modifications and clarifications of the first agreement.[38]

To the first four "General Provisions" which were maintained was added an inclusion of Article 29 of the Mexican Federal Labor Law. Previously, this Article had been mentioned only by name; now, the actual wording of Article 29 was written into the new agreement as it pertained to Mexican foreign labor living expenses, transportation, and repatriation. Under the section dealing with "transportation", the revised agreement referred specifically to the guarantees spelled out in Article 29.

Contained within the key section regarding "Wages and Employment" there were additional changes. The April agreement provided that Mexicans receive the same wage as other groups "under the same conditions within the same area." Both agreements guaranteed that approval would have to be obtained from the worker and the Mexican Government before non-agricultural work was allowed. In addition, the revised agreement of April, 1943, prevented arbitrary geographical displacement

17

of Mexican workers "with(out) the express approval of the worker and ... the ... Mexican Government."

Another revision dealt with the provision for hygienic lodgings, medical and sanitary services.[39] The first agreement vaguely stated that these services be identical to those received by domestic workers without stipulating that Mexicans be given those services without charge. Now, Mexican workers were promised these "without cost".

The revised agreement reinforced and extended the power of Mexican authorities to inspect Mexican farm working conditions in the United States. Mexican Labor Inspectors, in addition to previously allowed Mexican Consuls, were promised "free access to the places of work of the Mexican workers." The FSA, which was still in charge of the program, was responsible for insuring that American growers would permit periodic Mexican inspection.

Although there was no change in the guarantee of a $3.00 per day unemployment compensation for all days over 25% of the period, there was a change in compensation for unemployment under 25% of the contract period. The first agreement stated that the latter compensation would be "on the same bases" as that provided for Americans; the new agreement stated that Mexicans, if laid off under 25% of the contract period, would "receive lodging and subsistence without cost to them"

The final change specified that the Wells Fargo Bank and Union Trust Company of San Francisco would keep the Mexican savings deposits until transferred to the Mexican Agricultural Credit Bank.

The April, 1943, agreement was important, for it signified the diplomatic power of Mexico. Mexico wanted explicit mention of Article 29. They got it. They wanted tougher provisions promising that braceros would receive the same wages as domestic labor. They got it. Every change was a stronger guarantee of Mexican Nationals' rights. The agreement of April 26, 1943, would set a pattern for further Mexican severings of the bracero program followed by United States pleas for resumption and ultimately a new agreement. This cycle of suspension, negotiation, new agreement repeats itself throughout the alien labor program of the 1940s and early 1950s.

The demise of the Farm Security Administration occurred in 1946, but its leadership of the Mexican Farm Labor Transportation Program ended in 1943.[40] On March 26, 1943, Chester C. Davis was appointed Administrator of Food Production and Distribution. This agency became the War Food Administration on April 19, 1943. In March, 1943, the War Food Administration assumed command of the agricultural labor program.

Public Law 45, which Congress passed on April 29, 1943, appropriated $26,100,000 for continuing the alien farm labor program under the direction of the War Food Administration and the Extension Service of the Department of Agriculture. Public Law 45 represented a stunning defeat for FSA policies. The law prohibited federal financial involvement in the transport of domestic workers from one country to another; the FSA had been involved in intrastate movements of workers to avoid needless hiring of foreign labor and to alleviate domestic unemployment since June, 1942.[41]

According to section 4(a):

> No part of the funds ... shall be expended for the transporta-
> tion of any worker from the county where he resides ... to a
> place of employment outside of such a county without the prior
> consent ... of the county extension agent ... if such worker has
> resided in such county for a ... year or more ... and has been
> engaged in agricultural labor.

The FSA was also defeated in its attempt to secure federal protective
legislation for the domestic rural poor. Section 4(b) stated that:

> No part of the funds ... shall be used directly or indirectly
> to fix, regulate, or impose minimum wages of housing standards,
> to regulate hours of work, or to impose or enforce collective
> bargaining requirements or union membership.[42]

Yet, Public Law 45 continued to recognize protection for foreign workers as provided under international agreement.

Section 5(g) contained the most dramatic reversal of the bilateralism of
the FSA sponsored program. One could interpret this section to indicate that Mexicans could be legally imported by non-government personnel across an "open border",
without any regulations. This situation, if exploited, could contravene any international controls by reestablishing the First World War system of United States
farmers raiding Mexico for its workers.

Section 5(g) empowered the Commissioner of Immigration and Naturalization with the approval of the Attorney General to regulate alien worker traffic.
Furthermore, Section 5(g) stipulated that only an identification card "with photo-
graph and fingerprints" would be required for entry. What about the internationally guaranteed worker contracts? What about the Mexican Government participation
in the program? The immediate result was private labor recruitment of Mexicans
in Arizona and Texas with 1,500 entering El Paso, Texas, in a single day in May,
1943.[43]

In the future, the illegal entry of wetbacks would intensify; sensational
episodes of recruitment and mistreatment by selfish-minded agricultural interests
would be revealed. Regardless of the officially expressed intent of Section 5(g),
the State Department indicated that farmers would recruit only if "the other Government (Mexico) involved had no objections"--this section contributed to the overall
denial of executive regulation and centralization of the Mexican farm labor program.[44]

April, 1943, marked the official end of the Mexican Farm Labor Transportation Program with the removal of the FSA and the substitution of the War Food Administration's Office of Labor as the principal agency in control of the bracero program.
The Mexican Farm Labor Transportation Program had been financed through a grant from
the President's Emergency Fund to the FSA totalling $1,169,020.23.[45] When the execu-
tive branch sought to extend indefinitely the temporary nature of the agreement it
had to seek long-term congressional financing. This opened up the possibility for
congressional emasculation and alteration of the program. Increasingly, Congress
would influence alien labor policy while the Executive would lose its initial power
to dominate and direct the program.

19

Footnotes:

1. NYT, June 1, 1941.

2. Wayne D. Rasmussen, A History of the Emergency Farm Labor Supply Program 1943-47 (Washington, 1951), p. 13.

3. Ibid., p. 14.

4. Ibid., p. 19.

5. Ibid.

6. NYT, September 30, 1941.

7. NYT, June 5, 1941.

8. NYT, November 16, 1941.

9. Ibid.

10. Rasmussen, History, p. 200.

11. Robert C. Jones, Mexican War Workers in the United States: The Mexico-United States Manpower Recruiting Program and Its Operation (Washington: Pan American Union, 1945), p. 2.

12. Ibid., p. 1, and Rasmussen, History, p. 200.

13. Up to July 9, 1942, there was a request for a total of 37,680 Mexican laborers. Leading groups who wanted alien labor were the sugar interets, California farmers, and the railroads. The Southern Pacific requested 5,000; California Field Crops, Inc., requested 4,000; Great Western Sugar Company wanted 3,800; Amalgamated Sugar, 2,750; and the farmers of Imperial County, California, desired 2,000. Their requests were prior to the first binational agreement of August, 1942. See: Mexican Folder, War Manpower Commission, Bureau of Placement and Rural Industries Division (RG211), National Archives.

14. Otey M. Scruggs, "The Evolution of the Farm Labor Agreement of 1942", Agricultural History, 34 (July 1970), p. 144.

15. Ibid.

16. 56 Stat. 1759-1769.

17. Rasmussen, History, pp. 201-02.

18. Scruggs, "Agreement of 1942", p. 143.

19. Ibid.

20. 56 Stat. 1765

21. 56 <u>Stat.</u> 1764. Italics added.

22. 56 <u>Stat.</u> 1764.

23. Press Conference, Franklin D. Roosevelt, October 20, 1942, microfilm at Harry S. Truman Library. For additional Rooseveltian descriptions of the military incentives behind the bracero program see: <u>The Public Papers and Addresses of Franklin D. Roosevelt</u>, 12, 175-78.

24. The agreement of August 4, 1942, is in 56 <u>Stat.</u> 1766-69.

25. ICFR, 1941 <u>Supp.</u>, p. 234.

26. Ten per cent became the amount of income that was transferred to a Mexican bank but the 1942 agreement did not specify the percentage of income that was deducted.

27. Otey M. Scruggs, "The Bracero Program Under the Farm Security Administration, 1942-1943," <u>Labor History</u>, 3 (Spring, 1962), p. 149.

28. <u>NYT</u>, April 26, 1943. There is a slight difference in the figures given by Mexico and the United States. The Secretaria de Gobernacion lists 4,152 workers who came to the United States in 1942, while the Department of Agriculture accounts for 4,189. Except for 1942, Mexican statistics are consistently higher than USDA statistics. See also: Ernesto Lopez Malo, "La Emigracion de Trabajadores Mexicanos", <u>Ciencias Sociales</u> (Washington, 1954), p. 220.

29. <u>NYT</u>, April 26, 1943: <u>Consolidated Progress Report of the Mexican Farm Labor Transportation Program of the Farm Security Administration</u>, December 20, 1942, pp. 2-12. The first legally contracted Mexican was Fausto Huet.

30. 56 <u>Stat.</u> 1766.

31. <u>NYT</u>, August 7, 1942. Although the FSA managed the Mexican Farm Labor Transportation Program, it cooperated with the United States Employment Service and State and County Department of Agriculture War Boards.

32. <u>NYT</u>, September 15, 1942.

33. <u>NYT</u>, August 7, 1942. Quotation from joint statement of Paul V. McNutt, head of the War Manpower Commission, and Secretary Wickard.

34. Allen J. Matusow, <u>Farm Policies and Politics in the Truman Years</u> (Cambridge: Harvard University Press, 1967), p. 69. For American Farm Bureau attack and general treatment of the Farm Security Administration, see Grant McConnell, <u>The Decline of Agrarian Democracy</u> (Berkeley: University of California Press, 1953), pp. 84, 88-111; George S. McGovern, ed., <u>Agricultural Thought in the Twentieth Century</u> (Indianapolis: Bobbs-Merrill, 1967), pp. 190-91, 354-55.

35. Scruggs, "Bracero Program", pp. 153, 158.

36. Carey McWilliams, "They Saved the Crops", The Inter-American, 2 (August, 1943), p. 13. Most of the men recruited were between the ages of 20 and 30. See Ernesto Lopez Malo, "Emigracion", pp. 220-27, for a passionate indictment of the alien labor program by a Mexican economist.

37. Scruggs, "Bracero Program", pp. 157-59

38. The Agreement of April 26, 1943, is found in U. S. Department of State, Executive Agreement Series 351, pp. 7-13.

39. The August, 1942, agreement referred to them as "Housing conditions, sanitary and medical services."

40. McConnell, The Decline, p. 97.

41. For Public Law 45 (House Joint Resolution 96) see 57 Stat. 70-73. PL 45 passed the Congress on April 16, 1943, and Roosevelt signed it on April 29, 1943.

42. Ibid.

43. McWilliams, "They Saved the Crops", p. 14.

44. Scruggs, "Bracero Program", p. 166.

45. Jones, War Workers, p. 5.

CHAPTER III

MEXICANS ON THE RAILROADS

United States railroad companies utilized the services of Mexican labor from 1943 to 1946. This railroad component of bracero labor rivaled the agricultural component in terms of numbers of agencies involved and intensity of both Mexican-United States and union-management disputes. Both the farm and non-farm bracero programs were wartime emergency measures, but unlike the agricultural bracero program, which did not end until 1965, the non-farm program terminated within a year after the allied victory over Japan in the Second World War. There were fewer Mexican nationals employed in railroad labor than there were in farm labor, but with over a hundred thousand Mexicans working on American railroads, the railroad component was an important aspect of the Mexican wartime labor program.

There was rising pressure from the railroads which culminated in the signing of a binational United States-Mexican agreement on April 29, 1943, allowing temporary employment of Mexican railroad workers. In the latter part of 1941, the Southern Pacific Railroad Company requested permission from the Immigration and Naturalization Service to hire Mexican citizens for maintenance-of-way work.[1] As with the pre-war requests for farm labor, there was widespread union opposition and solid governmental reluctance to import foreign labor.

The Southern Pacific announced in May, 1942, that there were a thousand unfilled positions which only Mexican contract labor could fill.[2] As of July 9, 1942, the Southern Pacific had requested a total of 5,000 Mexican laborers.[3] It was not until September, 1942, almost a year after the railroad's first request, that the War Manpower Commission, which operated the railroad labor importation program, began to investigate seriously the Southern Pacific's alleged domestic labor shortages. The War Manpower Commission directed its state directors in California, Oregon, Nevada, Texas, Arizona and Utah to certify whether a labor shortage existed on the Southern Pacific. The state directors concluded that a labor shortage did exist but was attributable to low wages and rigid hiring specifications.[4]

A labor-management conference met in Chicago in October, 1942, to develop a joint proposal for importing Mexican railroad labor. The conference presented its recommendations to the Management-Labor Policy Committee of the War Manpower Commission in November.[5] The Management-Labor Policy Committee concluded that a "critical (labor) situation on certain railroads" existed and recommended that "the necessary steps to secure the importation of such track workers be taken at once."[6] The Policy Committee acted favorably on the recommendations and on December 16, 1942, requested from the Secretary of State that he proceed to negotiate an agreement with the Mexican Government to import railroad labor.

Negotiations which lead to an international agreement between the United States and Mexico began on January 29, 1943, when Ambassador George S. Messersmith sent a note requesting international discussions on the importation of Mexican track labor to the United States. Ezequial Padilla, Mexican Foreign Minister, responded favorably on February 3, 1943.[7] In April Arthur W. Motley, who served as the negotiating representative of Paul V. McNutt, Chairman of the War Manpower Commission, joined the State Department team in Mexico.[8] A tentative agreement was reached April 13, 1943, and was consummated through an exchange of notes on April 29, 1943, in Mexico City, between the Mexican Ministry of Foreign Affairs and the United States Embassy.[9]

Under the terms of the intergovernmental agreement, Mexican railroad labor was exempted from United States military service, guaranteed nondiscriminatory treatment and accorded the migrant worker guarantees of Article 29 of the Mexican Federal Labor Law.[10] The employer was also required to issue a bond equal to the repatriation costs in order to ensure the return of Mexican workers. The agreement further stipulated that Mexican labor could not be employed to displace either domestic labor, to depress the wage scales, or to adversely affect the general conditions of labor.

The international agreement specified that the individual worker contracts were written in both Spanish and English. The United States, represented by the War Manpower Commission, had to sign a contract with both Mexican worker and United States employer, with the latter being defined as the operator of a non-agricultural enterprise.

The United States Public Health Service and Mexican public health authorities provided physical examinations for each prospective worker. Although both countries had to certify the fitness of each Mexican national Mexico determined the total number of railroad workers admitted to the United States after receiving United States requests for workers.

Commensurate with Article 29 of the Mexican Labor Law, the agreement levied all costs accrued in the conveyance of workers to and from the Mexican point of contract origin upon the United States. Although the State Department accepted ultimate responsibility for the costs of transportation, personal effects and immigration regulations, the United States, in accordance with the agreement, arranged for the employer to pay these expenses, while recognizing that "this (referring to the potential costs to the employer) does not diminish the scope of the obligations (of) the United States Government."[11]

The agreement outlined several regulations concerning wages and employment conditions. Mexican wages were to equal domestic wages for the same work; the prevailing hourly wage was to be no lower than forty-six cents an hour. Job transfers were extremely difficult to obtain: "Any change to another type of work within this classification shall be made only with the express approval of the worker and with the consent of the Mexican Government."[12] Workers could purchase goods and services at places of their own choosing. Mexican workers were guaranteed the same quality of housing, food, sanitation and medical care as United States workers employed in similar occupations in the same area.[13]

24

Mexican workers could unionize and bargain collectively with the proviso that their labor spokesmen were from Mexican railroad labor ranks. If able and willing to work, Mexican non-agricultural workers were guaranteed 90% full-time employment throughout their contract period and 75% employment for a specific pay period. Each contract period was for six months, although this was not spelled out in the agreement. The worker was guaranteed an average of 90% employment for the six months. A particular pay period, say one week, could find him working only 75% of the time as long as the average of all the pay periods totalled 90%.

The pact provided for some measure of investigating compliance. Mexican Consuls and Mexican field inspectors were authorized to inspect places of employ periodically and investigate complaints. The War Manpower Commission guaranteed their freedom of action and acted upon complaints.

The agreement in principle permitted the renewal of contracts but specific details were not enunciated until after the labor program had begun. The Mexican-United States pact proclaimed that unless a contract was renewed, the prolonged stay of a Mexican national was illegal and in violation of the immigration laws.

Similar to the binational agricultural worker agreement of August, 1942, there was a provision that a portion of the Mexican's salary would be deposited automatically into a savings fund. The intent was to guarantee the worker some capital upon returning to Mexico. The War Manpower Commission was responsible for the maintenance of these savings funds until they were credited to the Banco Ahorro Nacional, S. A. International disagreement arose over Mexico's insistence that railroad laborers be granted the option of purchasing United States agricultural implements with their savings funds; Mexicans doing farm work in the United States had been allowed to do so under the terms of the August, 1942, Mexican-United States agricultural worker agreement. Mexico wanted the United States to "grant export permits and priorities for agricultural implements in an amount equal to the total of the workers' savings funds."[14] The State Department adamantly objected, contending that the production priorities of the Second World War precluded an adequate amount of agricultural implements for domestic use. There was no reference made to agricultural implements in the April, 1943 agreement. State also succeeded in thwarting Mexican demands for life insurance guarantees and a quasi-social security program.[15]

Although the two principal agencies in this area were the War Manpower Commission and the Railroad Retirement Board, there were a number of other governmental, union and railroad agencies involved in the Mexican railroad labor importation program. The Department of Justice through its Immigration and Naturalization Service and its Board of Immigration Appeals authorized the temporary admission of Mexican non-agricultural workers pursuant to the ninth proviso to Section Three of the 1917 Immigration Act. This proviso, which provided legal justification for bringing in both Mexican farm and non-farm workers in the 1940s, stated that "the Commissioner General of Immigration with the approval of the Secretary of Labor shall issue rules and prescribe conditions, including exaction of such bonds as may be necessary, to control and regulate the admission and return of otherwise inadmissible aliens applying for temporary admission."[16] The Board of Immigration Appeals had the initial authority to determine whether non-agricultural Mexican employment be used solely for maintenance of way work.[17]

The Office of Price Administration issued food and shoe stamps as part of the recruitment process in Mexico. Food stamps were issued to those who did not eat at railroad commissaries. OPA stopped these issuances before the termination of the program in 1946.[18]

As previously mentioned, neither nation wanted to export or import sick workers. The United States Public Health Service provided physical examinations for every recruited worker. Other agencies involved in the railroad labor program were the Treasury Department, which was consulted on tax matters, and the Department of State, which served as the chief diplomatic negotiating agency in the formation of the binational agreement and assisted in distributing Mexican workers to the railroads.[19]

Another important agency was the Office of Defense Transportation. Its duties were to "sponsor (the) influx of Mexican workers for railroad jobs ... in the West"; to act as an auxiliary agency in utilizing Mexican workers with appropriate skills for repair yard jobs; "to determine the extent to which imported labor is the answer to unskilled labor needs and to analyze how Mexican workers can be used in other occupational classes."[20] ODT's Director, Joseph B. Eastman, was active in requesting labor for western railroads, demanding Mexican compliance with agreements, and in providing train cars for repatriation.[21]

Other agencies involved in this labor program were associated railroad companies among which were the Association of American Railroads, Western Association of Railway Executives, and dozens of individual railroad companies which contracted Mexican labor. The prominent labor organizations actively involved in the Mexican labor importation program for railroads were the Brotherhood of Maintenance of Way Employees, the Railway Labor Executives' Association, the Brotherhood of Railway and Steamship Clerks, and the Railway Employees' Department, American Federation of Labor.[22]

The War Manpower Commission was the key agency involved with the operations of the Mexican railroad labor program. The War Manpower Commission's Employment Office Service Division of the Bureau of Placement directed the program until April, 1944, when the newly created Foreign Labor Section of the Bureau of Placement assumed overall responsibility. The WMC directed this labor program until the former's abolition on September 19, 1945, when many of its alien labor departments such as the United States Employment Service, the Foreign Labor Section, and the Rural Industries Division were transferred to the Department of Labor.[23]

Chairman McNutt issued regulations indicating his agency's broad powers of administration.[24] The WMC supervised the selection of Mexican workers and made arrangements for their entry into the United States. The Commission served as the principal agent of the United States in entering into contracts with each Mexican worker and each American employer as provided in the international agreement of April, 1943. The Commission was further authorized to utilize the personnel and facilities of the Railroad Retirement Board, the second most powerful agency which managed the Mexican non-farm importation program. The WMC was empowered to administer "all other operational aspects" of the non-farm labor program.[25]

The War Manpower Commission appointed a representative to act as a liason with the Mexican Government. This representative was entrusted with broad administrative powers and surpassed the United States Embassy as the principal United States railroad labor agency in Mexico. On April 28, 1943, the Commission appointed Samuel B. Hough as its first representative; he served from April 28, 1943, to March 26, 1945. At this time Churchill Murray replaced him and assumed his duties until June, 1946, when the alien railroad labor program ended.

The Commission's representative directed "all contacts" with Mexico which pertained to the railroad agreement with the United States. He was in charge of "all negotiations and arrangements" with the United States Department of Public Health, the Immigration and Naturalization Service, and the Office of Price Administration. The general execution of worker-government contracts was under his jurisdiction, yet the representative delegated "routine execution of contracts" to the Railroad Retirement Board. The Railroad Retirement Board served as an enforcement agency in Mexico by implementing the representative's orders and proclamations. Early in the program, the WMC clarified the important but secondary role of the RRB. In spite of its many and varied powers, several WMC directives referred directly to the secondary relationship of the RRB. This was stated laconically in correspondence between Lawrence A. Appley, Executive Director, War Manpower Commission, to Murray W. Latimer, Chairman of the Railroad Retirement Board. The WMC representative "will represent the interests of ... the ...Railroad Retirement Board in all matters relating to coordination of the ... recruitment program."[26]

The representative of the WMC coordinated his non-agricultural labor recruitment with the farm labor program of the Farm Security Administration. Hough did not interfere with FSA attempts to achieve its recruitment quotas or to acquire a sufficient number of railroad cars for the transferral of farm workers.[27] If the WMC representative used FSA office space, telephones, secretarial services or telegraph services, the latter agency was reimbursed.[28] Clearly, the farm worker recruitment machinery was established first and the WMC scrupulously avoided inter-agency rivalry between farm and non-farm worker programs. The potential quantity of legally contracted Mexican nationals was not infinite and in order to avoid chaotic counterproductive rivalry, it was deemed essential that a spirit of cooperation exist between United States foreign labor agencies in the initial days of both farm and non-farm recruitment programs.

The War Manpower Commission assumed an equally important role in the Mexican railroad labor program in the United States. Complaints regarding individual work agreements between the foreign worker and the United States or employer agreements between the government and the railroads were ultimately settled by the WMC. The Commission was in charge of work transfers between railroads which did not entail a change of occupation and informed the RRB of any terminations of employment.[29] Essentially, the WMC was the administrator of the labor program and the chief enforcer of compliance with international agreements and internationally approved contracts. Although the WMC retained ultimate power in the recruitment and placement phases of the war worker operation, the RRB was actively involved in these areas.

The Railroad Retirement Board had numerous specific duties. The RRB lent its clerical services to the Immigration and Naturalization Service as well as to the United States Public Health Service.[30] The RRB negotiated with American railroads concerning, first, the specifications and requirements for the supply of workers; secondly, adequate food and transportation facilities during the emigration and repatriation of workers; and third, the provisions for adequate housing, sanitary and medical facilities as guaranteed in the agreement. The Board had the responsibility of recruiting and processing workers for the railroad industry. The Board determined worker qualifications and handled details concerning interviewing, the selection of workers and with the approval of the WMC representative, issued Individual Work Agreements and Selection Cards. The Board assisted in allocating workers among the railroad companies and filled predetermined quotas of workers with Mexicans approved for maintenance-of-way work. The RRB was responsible for specific operations of the Mexican recruitment center; the WMC was the general supervisor.[31]

Each worker received an Individual Work Agreement defining specific wage rates, housing conditions and medical care that the worker was entitled to receive. Both the RRB and WMC informed the worker of his rights. The RRB scheduled trains, supervised the departure of Mexicans and provided train riders to inspect directly the actual transportation of Mexican farm workers to the United States. The Board reported all contractual violations committed by the railroads during the worker's voyage and any failure of a worker to reach his destination to the WMC. Each employer was compelled to keep current employment records of every foreign worker as devised by the RRB with the approval of the WMC. The WMC instructed the railroad companies to notify the RRB of any incidents of worker non-performance for seven consecutive days or of separation from his employer.[32]

The WMC and the RRB were careful in screening potential employers and certifying a labor shortage before importing Mexican non-farm workers. The WMC erected an intricate procedure prior to allowing railroads to use foreign workers. Railroad companies' applications for alien labor had to be approved by the WMC, RRB and the Brotherhood of Maintenance of Way Employees.[33]

Railroads could not hire foreign workers unless the supply of domestic workers was inadequate and recruitment attempts of the United States Employment Service and the Railroad Retirement Board Employment Service had failed.[34] Unions vigorously charged that the domestic railroad labor shortage was perpetuated within a high unemployment economy by outrageously low wages. George E. McNulty, Acting General Chairman, Brotherhood of Maintenance of Way Employees, Burlington System Division, trenchantly remarked that had American workers "received nearly the wages that were paid in other industries for comparable work, there would have been no necessity for importation of foreign labor."[35] Elmer E. Milliman, President of the Brotherhood of Maintenance of Way Employees, in a tersely worded letter to Secretary of Labor Lewis B. Schwellenbach, asserted that thousands of Americans refused maintenance-of-way employment because of low wages. Milliman referred to domestic railroad working conditions as a "national disgrace when workers receive such sub-standard rates of pay in the greatest service industry in this country."[36]

These assertions that better pay for domestic labor was the cure-all for filling labor shortages in the railroad industry were substantiated in large part by RRB statistics.[37]

REFUSAL OF APPLICANTS TO ACCEPT MAINTENANCE OF
WAY JOBS ON RAILROADS BECAUSE OF LOW WAGES
DURING THE PERIOD SEPTEMBER 17 TO
SEPTEMBER 29, 1945

By Occupations

Occupations	Number Offered Referral	Number Refused Referral	Percent of Refusals
Track Laborers	7,046	2,550	36.2
B&B Carpenters	455	239	52.5
B&B Painters	387	149	38.5
B&B Helpers	916	380	41.5
B&B Laborers	426	223	52.3
Other M. of W. Workers	317	108	34.1
Total	9.547	3,649	38.2

By Railroad Retirement Board Regions

	Number Offered Referral	Number Refused Referral	Percent of Refusals
Atlanta	1,322	316	23.9
New York	1,323	939	71.0
Cleveland	1,461	463	32.0
Chicago	1,071	648	60.5
Dallas	327	82	25.0
Kansas City	1,608	574	35.7
Minneapolis	553	182	33.0
Denver	943	156	16.5
San Francisco	939	289	30.7
Total	9,547	3,649	38.2

October 23, 1945, Office of War Mobilization and Reconversion Folder, Office of the Secretary, Department of Labor (RG 174), NA. Wage rate was 57¢ an hour. Some had to work 60 hours before getting overtime pay of time and a half.

Regional directors reported astonishing rates of job refusals from those offered employment. In the New York City Region, 71% refused maintenance-of-way employment due to low wages; in Chicago, 60% refused; in San Francisco, 30.7% refused; and in Dallas, 25% declined employment. Between September 17, 1945, and September 29, 1945, when demobilization of American troops began to swell the labor force, 7,046 Americans, of whom many were unemployed, were offered track labor positions with 2,550 or 36.2% refusing employment. In this same national sample, 52.5% of those domestic laborers offered carpenter railroad work refused and the percentage of refusals for railroad painting work reached 38.5%.[38] These applicants stated specifically that low wages precluded any possible incentives for employment. The unions' accusations and the RRB's own statistics strongly indicate that much of the importation of Mexican labor for railroad work could have been reduced or eliminated with higher wages for American labor.

The WMC and the RRB should not be held directly responsible for eliminating the intrinsic cause of a domestic railroad labor shortage. These two agencies were not able to force United States citizens to accept undesirable employment or to compel the railroads to raise their wages. In spite of these agencies' wide latitude of powers, setting domestic wage rates was not one of them. The international agreement merely stated that the minimum hourly wage rate for Mexicans was forty-six cents an hour or higher if necessary to equal domestic wages for comparable labor. A domestic minimum wage rate was established in 1944 at fifty-seven cents an hour retroactive to February 1, 1943.[39] The above statistics reflect refusals after the establishment of this rate; this rate was also established when the Mexican national railroad labor program was well underway. It is significant, regardless of who is to blame, that the entire labor importation program could have been obviated had there been an adequate domestic minimum wage rate for railroad labor.

Railroad companies were obligated to sign an agreement, "Contracts to Employ and Transportation Agreements", with the United States before hiring Mexican national labor. There were many items in these government-to-railroad agreements that bound the railroads to comply with the employment condition guarantees of the binational agreement as well as others devised by the WMC. Railroads could not reject workers whom the RRB recruited in Mexico. There were provisions which were seldom exercised for the railroad companies to conduct their own physical examinations in Mexico at their own expense. Instead, they generally accepted the findings of the United States Public Health Service.[40] In addition, the railroads had to prepare a Selection Card for each worker designating the specific location of employment; railroads had to guarantee the Mexicans a minimum wage which rose from 46¢ to 57¢ an hour and paid the overtime rate of an hour and a half for work performed beyond eight hours a day.[41] The government-to-railroad agreement required railroads to begin employing their workers the day after they arrived at the work camp. The agreement reiterated the railroads' obligations to pay round trip transportation expenses. Should a Mexican railroad worker desire repatriation due to illness, homesickness, unhappiness or discharge from employment, the railroad had to remunerate the worker for his return trip.[42]

Concerning the posting of a bond, the employer-to-government agreement specified that the employer must pay a $20 bond which ensured each worker's return to Mexico. This bond covered a maximum liability of $500 for each non-returning worker and was returned to the railroad upon the arrival of the Mexican to Mexico.[43]

The railway either performed its contractual obligations or faced possible censure and loss of alien labor. If a railroad company failed to compensate the worker for salary, transportation or subsistence, the United States Government had to pay the difference but demanded reimbursement at an annual interest rate of six per cent. These agreements were between unequal partners: "Any questions as to the railway's liability or rights or obligations are to be determined by the War Manpower Commission in accordance with regulations prescribed by the Chairman of the Commission."[44]

The government also signed agreements with each individual worker. The binational agreement required such contracts. These worker agreements demonstrated Mexico's desire for direct United States supervision of Mexican nationals' working conditions. Even though Mexico was content to assist American labor, allegedly depleted through a world war, its assistance was conditional upon United States supervision. In the worker agreements, the minimum wage was again defined, as was the overtime rate. The worker was morally committed to work for 180 days except for Sundays and holidays but at his discretion could legally sever his Individual Work Agreement with the United States.45

Both the worker-to-government agreement and railroad-to-government agreement declared in principle that the WMC was to settle complaints of either employer or employee. The WMC elucidation of this complex grievance machinery was stated in various regulations.46 Complaints of either employer or employee concerning agreement non-compliance were filed with the local employment office of the WMC or with a representative of the RRB. The manager of the WMC local employment office made the initial determination of any conflict, was authorized to make any necessary investigations, and was required to personally hear testimony of both worker and railroad. Either laborer or railroad could appeal the local manager's decision within three days to the nearest WMC area or state director. As with the local employment office he then held a hearing which included both parties to the dispute.

The Area Management-Labor War Manpower Committee would suggest names to the area or state director, who would then select a hearing panel composed equally of management and labor representatives. This panel was advisory in nature; it recommended to the area or state director what the determination should be, with the director making the ultimate decision on the appeal. This intricate appeals bureaucracy permitted further appeals to the nearest Regional Director of the WMC. The Regional Director could sustain, stay or alter any previous appeal decision. The Chairman of the WMC could resolve the labor dispute with or without the concurrence of the Regional Director involved. If a worker lost his case at the Area Director level and chose to appeal to the Regional Director or Chairman, he had to do so within three days or face at least temporary separation from the railroad. If the appeal was punctual, a worker who might have lost an earlier appeal was entitled to continue working until ultimate determination had been made.

Since the binational agreement provided that Mexican nationals could seek union membership and bargain collectively, WMC Regulation Number 6 reaffirmed that the worker could utilize union aid during the appeal process. Generally, those unions which accepted Mexican national membership participated casually and ineffectively "in the recruiting program and (in) the solution of problems arising under it."47

Most of the Mexican workers imported under the terms of the non-agricultural agreement performed railroad work. The first of these Mexican railroad workers arrived in the United States on May 10, 1943. Between May 13, 1943, when the first train left Mexico City and June 15, 1943, 6,000 laborers arrived, with 3,500 going to the Southern Pacific; 2,200 working for the Atchison, Topeka and Santa Fe; and 300 destined for the Western Pacific. Both the international agreement and the Attorney General's specific authorization on May 6, 1943, made this possible.48 These 6,000 workers were exported on eight train convoys. They departed from

Buena Vista Station in Mexico City for Guadalajara, El Paso, Texas or Nogales, Arizona. They arrived on either Mexican carrier or the Southern Pacific. The National Railways of Mexico described a typical journey for the first braceros admitted to the United States under the non-farm labor program:

> A special train made up of twelve first class coaches of the Southern Pacific, a dining car of the same line and a dining car of the National Railways of Mexico will leave Buenavista at 10:00 A.M. May 29 (1943) bearing 750 workers destined to Guadalajara with the understanding that this rolling stock will be turned over to the S.P. of Mexico for the trip north.[49]

The arrival of these Mexicans stimulated strong United States statements applauding hemispheric solidarity and promising to protect Mexico's own economic necessities. Joseph Eastman declared that "transportation is the blood brother of production and modern warfare" and extolled the bracero program's contribution to the war.[50] Arthur Motley, now Acting Director of the WMC Bureau of Placement, described the program as one of "valuable action" in lending "assistance on our home front".[51] Paul V. McNutt declared that Mexico made a "direct and much needed contribution to the war production program of this country and the United Nations."[52] Aware of Mexico's desire to bolster its own economy, McNutt announced that the United States would import only unskilled labor whose departure would not be detrimental to Mexico's economy.[53] Mexico had proven a conscientious negotiator in securing legal protection for its citizens, and good politics, if not underlying humanitarian impulses, dictated a foreign policy which was cognizant of Mexico's reluctance in having its labor drained off or mistreated.

A supplemental certification for an additional 9,360 workers was made on June 15, 1943. This brought to 15,360 the number of Mexican railroad employees in the United States by August, 1943. In addition to the Southern Pacific, Atchison, Topeka and Santa Fe and the Western Pacific, which were allotted 4,200 extra workers, other railroads were brought into this international worker program. These were the Texas Pacific (400 workers), the Chicago, Rock Island and Pacific (300 workers), the Spokane, Portland and Seattle (275 workers), the Northwestern Pacific (200 workers) and the San Diego and Arizona Eastern (100 workers).[54]

In 1944 the recruitment process accelerated rapidly with Mexico approving quotas of 40,000 workers in March, 1944, and upwards to 50,000 in July, 1944. By April 1, 1944, 36,000 workers were being employed on twenty-four different railroads.[55] In May, 1944, 5,900 additional braceros arrived, which brought to twenty-nine the number of railroad companies employing Mexican maintenance-of-way labor.[56] Although most Mexicans worked in the West, the Pennsylvania Railroad and the New York Central ranked third and fourth respectively in the numbers of Mexicans hired by United States railroads. By 1945, 80,137 Mexicans had been delivered for railroad work. Over half of these Mexicans worked for the Southern Pacific and the Atchison, Topeka and Santa Fe.[57]

Within the first thirteen months of the program, 51,774 workers crossed the international boundary, with the majority laboring in western Montana, Washington, Oregon, California, Nevada and southern Arizona.[58] In the succeeding year,

58,091 were recruited and from April 1, 1945, to the cessation of recruitment in August, 1945, 35,540 arrived, making a grand total of 136,090.[59] Between April and June, 1945, 24,914 Mexican citizens emigrated to the United States-- the largest total for any quarter during the program's existence. In March, 1945, Mexicans were working for thirty-two different railroad companies and in August 1945, the banner month in terms of numbers of Mexicans in the United States, thirty-five separate railroads employed 69,000 workers.[60]

Japan's surrender on August 14, 1945, led to the demise of the railroad labor importation program. From its inception, the Mexican non-agricultural program had been intended to remedy a wartime emergency. After V-J Day, the initial rationale for the wartime bracero program ended and binational measures were subsequently taken to terminate the Mexican railroad labor importation program.

Churchill Murray, the WMC representative in Mexico, received instructions on August 16, 1945, to end recruiting and prevent any additional worker-to-government or railroad-to-government contracts from being issued. Those braceros who had already signed contracts but who had not departed for the United States would be allowed to do so. Each contract was for six months, which meant some contract expirations would not occur until February, 1946.

The post-V-J Day repatriation of Mexican workers created much bitterness and antagonism between United States government agencies, railroad companies and organized labor. Union groups and railroad companies were protagonists, while the United States Government was caught in the middle. The unions demanded immediate unconditional repatriation, while the railroads sought to delay it. The government was either criticized for being too recalcitrant in rapidly repatriating Mexicans or for being overzealous in ending the employment of Mexican railroad labor in this country.

As early as March 12, 1945, five months before the end of the Second World War, the WMC informed the railroads, "that upon cessation of military operations, recruitment and contract renewals would be discontinued immediately and that Mexican nationals would repatriated as soon as possible."[61] On August 23, 1945, the day after the WMC convoked a meeting with representatives from the RRB, ODT, State Department, railroads and union groups to devise repatriation policies, the railroads were told that contract renewals and all recruitment had been stopped. The railroads also received instructions concerning wage payments to repatriated workers, contract renewals and the settlement of claims prior to contract expiration.[62]

On August 25, 1946, the American Embassy received official confirmation from the State Department to wind down the program. The United States Public Health Service ordered its doctors to leave Mexico and the RRB began to dismantle its processing point at Queretaro and to dismiss its personnel throughout Mexico.[63]

The unions charged that both government and railroads were lackadaisical in repatriating workers. A. E. Lyon, Executive Secretary of the Railway Labor Executives' Association, charged the Labor Department with violating "definite assurances" that in exchange for union support and cooperation in the wartime labor importation program, Mexicans would be returned immediately upon the cessation of the conflict.

Lyon claimed that the railroads were purposely paying braceros low wages in order
to avoid hiring domestic labor while they were requesting that Mexican labor be
retained until adequate domestic labor became available.[64] The Brotherhood of
Maintenance of Way Employees disputed the railroads' contention that the prolongation of the return of Mexican nationals was due to an inadequate supply of railroad
cars. The union charged that immediately after V-J Day the railroads demanded renewal of all existing contracts before knowing how many cars would be available
and what effect returning United States soldiers would have on the labor market.[65]
The Brotherhood maintained that between 30,000 and 40,000 Mexicans were still in
the United States as of February, 1946, and that many Mexicans departed with feelings of bitter anti-Americanism because they were prevented from immediately returning to Mexico after the expiration of their contracts. In addition, unions
asserted that the postwar prolongation of Mexican labor competition in the United
States "resulted in ill feelings between Mexican nationals and domestic workers."[66]

The railroads' reluctance to repatriate and the lack of inter-agency cooperation in utilizing existing transportation facilities impeded rapid repatriation. Both the farm labor and non-farm labor programs required trains to repatriate Mexicans. Even though the intergovernmental farm labor program did not terminate until 1965, there was an immediate short-term repatriation effort after the
Second World War which competed for railroad space with the non-farm program. The
problem of inadequate transportation facilities became so acute that John W. Snyder,
the Director of War Mobilization and Reconversion, appointed an inter-agency task
force committee to investigate the problem. On the committee were representatives
of the War Manpower Commission, the Office of Defense Transportation, the Department of Agriculture, the Department of State and the Department of Labor, with
Robert C. Goodwin, Director of the United States Employment Service, serving
as Chairman.[67] Snyder personally recommended that the Department of Agriculture
use the bulk of the transportation equipment until November 20, 1945, after which
time only railroad workers would be repatriated through December 5, 1945. Thereafter, railway and farm workers would be exported equally.[68] The result of Snyder's
suggestions was the repatriation of 15,212 railwaymen in December, 1945; 12,623 in
January, 1946; and 10,533 in February, with the rest returned by the late spring
of 1946.[69]

There were many instances which lent credence to union charges of excessive delay. In May, 1945, 497 Mexicans were imported; this was the month in which
Germany surrendered.[70] Recruitment reached its peak after V-E Day in August, 1945,
when the largest total of Mexican railroad workers were in the United States. The
Justice Department extended the stay of Mexicans from thirty days to six months after
the termination of hostilities.[71] Although the United States might have been justified in honoring six-month contracts signed just before the end of the war, how does
one explain the authorization which allowed a six-months' renewal of the above contracts after the war? As mentioned above, many Mexicans who had signed contracts
prior to V_J Day but who had not arrived in the United States were still allowed to
enter, resulting in further delays of total repatriation. It was not until the last
week in August, two weeks after V-J Day, when the last group of Mexicans, totalling
1,606, were admitted to the United States.[72] Repatriation between August 18 and
October 6, 1945, amounted to only 10,882 or approximately 1,550 a week.[73] With 8,000
contract renewals permitted after V-J Day, effective large-scale repatriation was
deferred until December, 1945.

There were 67,704 Mexicans servicing United States railroads on August 18, 1945, with an anticipated return rate of 7,500 a month. This latter figure was not arrived at until December. Surely the number of Mexican farm workers should not have precluded rapid repatriation of railroad workers, for there were only 35,000 legally contracted agricultural workers in the United States in October, 1945.[74] Despite the fact that this total represented only one-half the number of railroad workers, the Snyder recommendations and the Goodwin committee did not advocate a continuous majority proportion of railway space for returning Mexican railwaymen Even though there was never a sincere attempt to dismantle rapidly the farm labor program after the Second World War, the War Food Administration, which was one of the principal agencies involved in the farm labor program, requested that farm workers be granted 75% of existing railroad transportation equipment for repatriation.[75]

As early as ten months before the end of the war, in October, 1944, a State Department memorandum revealed that railroad workers might not be immediately returned to Mexico but would be used "until demobilization...provided domestic workers to ... industries ... using Mexican workers."[76] The memorandum stressed that a lack of speed was necessary in repatriating Mexican railroad workers, which was inconsistent with union demands that repatriation be completed shortly after the Second World War. The memorandum set at 7,000 the maximum monthly rate of return. Had this been followed, it would have meant the delay of total repatriation until mid-summer of 1946. The State Department memorandum accurately predicted that either farm or non-farm workers would remain for a longer period of time due to differing binational agreement renewals. The memorandum ruled out compulsory contract extensions after the war but indicated that two consenting parties, worker and employer, could renew their contracts after hostilities. Actually, the worker was not legally bound to honor his contract, which ruled out the remotest possibility of compulsory renewal or extension.[77] Not surprisingly, government agencies maintained a firm denial of laxity. Secretary of Labor L. B. Schwellenbach, as late as March 27, 1946, averred that the "policy of the Department of Labor has been to repatriate the Mexican railroad workers as rapidly as possible."[78]

Although it is difficult to determine what would have constituted sensible speed in repatriating braceros, it appears that the unions were correct in charging delay in tactics. Recruitment was intensified towards the end of the war, and during its immediate aftermath contracts were renewed. Mexican railroad labor was being exported to the United States weeks after the end of the war under a six-month contract period. The farm labor program was extended and therefore did not require so large a share of train facilities as it received for repatriation. There was little urgency in returning the Mexican railroad worker to his country.

It is questionable whether the United States railroads required bracero labor any more than the Mexican. The paramount reason for importing this labor was the state of disrepair of fixed railroad property such as track and bridges. The bracero was declared essential as a substitute for domestic labor which either departed from the railroad for the war or higher paying defense industries. There was never any inclination to keep the domestic worker on the railroad and train the Mexican in defense work; he was to perform an essential but grueling task of maintaining American railroads. It is questionable, however, whether United States railroad requirements were greater than the Mexican ones.

During the war, the Mexican railroad system was in a state of utter disarray, which demanded the same labor services being performed by Mexicans in the United States. The number of railroad accidents and breakdowns were at a record high and every Mexican railroad was in debt. Even after the nation took over most of the railroads in 1937, the latter went from a 19,000,000 peso profit to a 9,000,000 peso deficit. Many predicted the imminent collapse of the Mexican railway system in 1944. The United States rejuvenated the Mexican railroad by selling locomotives, roadbed equipment, and repair facilities, lending it management personnel and contributing "U.S. funds to employ extra workers and staff on the Nacionales to increase efficiency."[79] Yet, the United States was employing Mexican workers to perform the same type of labor that the United States was financing in Mexico.

A major union charged that the United States was running the Mexican railways in such a way as to prevent Mexican cooperation in lending its cars for repatriation.[80] Joseph B. Eastman, Chairman of the ODT, remarked that since the United States had offered "substantial aid in rehabilitating and improving its (the Mexican) railway system,...the Mexican Government should reciprocate by providing workers" to the United States.[81] It is incongruous for the United States to finance Mexican recruiting efforts which were insufficient in terms of Mexican requirements and simultaneously employ tens of thousands of Mexican railroad workers. In addition, how could the United States afford to assume the major burden of rebuilding the Mexican railroad when United States government agencies and railroad companies predicted the demise of the United States railroad unless bracero labor was imported? This is not to suggest that the United States should not have rendered valuable assistance to the Mexican railroad industry. The above merely focuses the irony of United States claims of a domestic railroad collapse while providing massive railroad assistance to Mexico. It also begs the question whether Mexicans were needed just as badly to work their own railroads as they were to maintain those of another nation.

The Mexican who voluntarily became a stranger in a foreign land experienced severe environmental change. He had to endure racial prejudice and physical hardships occasioned by the necessary adaptation to a warmer climate at a lower altitude. The food was different and his dietary habits conflicted with the United States diet. A dearth of Spanish-speaking railroad foremen or supervisors compounded his frustration. Many Mexicans were simply not accustomed to difficult manual labor; they resented their living quarters and many were not adequately informed of their legally guaranteed rights.[82]

Changing climate was particularly troublesome, the Dallas regional director of the RRB reported.[83] The railroads' medically unsound solution to heat prostration was to reduce the amount of cold drinking water, look for those Mexicans who prespired excessively, and give "particular and immediate attention to those who suddenly cease sweating."[84]

Mexicans could satisfy their dietary predilections only if they were transported to a distant Mexican market or if Mexican food were brought to them. The United States briefly contemplated a federally financed and operated program "to teach the imported Mexicans to cook, order food, and prepare balanced meals."[85] The Mexican-United States agreement provided that Mexicans could purchase any consumable items where they desired. The Mexican Ministry of Labor pressured WMC representative Churchill Murray into investigating an alleged New York Central practice of permitting Mexicans to purchase food outside the work camp only to charge them $1.20 a day for food which was not consumed.[86] On the Burlington Railroad, sixty-five to seventy workers expelled a cook and demanded a replacement.[87] Some railroads hired Mexicans to prepare the food or allowed Mexican workers to double as cooks. A few railroads taught United States cooks the art of Mexican cuisine. Basically, "there were no fixed standards of quantity, quality or charges for food."[88] Mexicans were guaranteed only the same quality and the same price as obtained for domestic labor.

Another Mexican grievance was one of racial discrimination. This problem became so acute on the Southern Pacific that its supervisors were cautioned against displaying racial bigotry.[89] Mexicans frequently encountered a United States foreman who was "a nervous, irritable, impatient type" who spoke little or no Spanish, and acted in a harsh and condescending manner.[90]

Mexico suspended the railroad labor program for several months beginning in August, 1943. No more Mexicans could enter the United States until certain demands were met. Mexico demanded an increase in bracero wages which would equal those of domestic labor. Many railroads claimed that this demand could not be fulfilled because they hired private contractors who in turn recruited domestic laborers. These contractors, who were paid directly by the railroad, hired urban labor at a higher wage rate than Mexican labor received.[91] The international agreement, however, made no exception for wage differentials between Mexican and privately contracted labor. The agreement stated that "wages paid to Mexican workers ... shall be the same as those paid for similar work to domestic workers at the place of employment." Mexico won a partial victory in 1944 when the hourly wage rate was increased from forty-six to fifty-seven cents.

Another contributing cause to the Mexican suspension of the bracero program was the lack of upward occupational mobility for Mexican railroad workers. Bracero advancement into better paying and higher skilled positions was virtually nonexistent. Postitions involving shop, warehouse and storehouse work were denied Mexicans whose initial job specification was track labor. With the lingering threat of permanent suspension, there emanated some concessions to Mexican demands for intra-industry transfer. The Justice Department ruled:

> It is ordered that the Mexican laborers ... may be employed
> ... in all classifications of "Laborer", "Helper", "Assistant
> Foreman", and semiskilled "Machine Operators".[92]

Previously, intra-industry occupational advances were allowed only under urgent job shortage emergencies.[93] Many railroads subsequently used the goal of job promotion as an incentive for greater bracero production and as an enticement for contract renewals. The WMC, the RRB, the Mexican Government and the appropriate United States labor organization had to approve each attempt to upgrade a worker's occupation.[94]

A third factor which precipitated Mexico's termination of the binational railroad labor program was the inability of braceros to leave one occupation for another. This restriction against inter-industry transfer prevented Mexicans from acquiring more than one trade. The United States through the Office of Defense Transportation assumed a non-compromising posture. ODT claimed that inter-industry mobility would prove calamitous to the bracero program because United States industry would not import aliens if there was a possibility of losing this labor to other industries. Chairman Eastman was a staunch opponent of inter-industry transfer: "Granting the Mexican request would be tantamount to ending all possibility of employing Mexican nationals in industries here."[95] Mexico, it appears, was not justified in this demand because she had previously denied United States requests for direct bracero hiring in non-ferrous metal mining, milling, smelting and refining industries.[96] Mexico feared that the result would be an exodus of miners, spurred on by higher United States wages, which would deplete the Mexican mining industry. Although Mexico would not allow direct hiring of its nationals by United States mining interests, Mexico desired inter-industry transfers after braceros arrived to the United States. The United States preferred direct importation into these occupations to pre-serve the credibility of the program. This battle between direct recruitment versus inter-occupational mobility raged without compromise. The diplomatic failure at compromise resulted in the United States outlawing work transfers between industries and Mexico maintaining restrictions against directly import-ing Mexicans for mining purposes.[97]

The problems the bracero encountered led to a strong bracero response in addition to that of his government. Mexican railroad workers went on strike against the Southern Pacific in Live Oak, California, in December, 1943. The Live Oak Strike dramatized the plight of the bracero in the United States. The incident which triggered the strike was the dismissal of Anastasio B. Cartes and Manuel M. Rivas, but the root causes of this strike were the following: first, braceros were transported to and from work in an uncovered truck; secondly, they received cold lunches instead of the usual hot lunch; third, they were sub-jected to unsanitary toilet facilities in their sleeping quarters; and four, there was insufficient heat in the old motel where they resided.[98]

The strike touched off a Railroad Retirement Board investigation which concluded that the Southern Pacific regarded bracero aspirations for better working conditions as politically inspired and agitative in nature.[99] Another RRB investigation verified that imported Mexican nationals in the Live Oak Strike "did not have electric lights in the washroom and had inadequate cess-pools." Cartes had been fired because he left work in order to clean his clothing before dark. The upshot of the sordid affair was the demand of twenty-nine Mexicans that either Cartes and Rivas be reinstated or they would terminate all bracero contracts in the Live Oaks region. In spite of government pressure on the Southern Pacific, there was no reinstatement, which resulted in the braceros walking off their jobs and returning to Mexico.[100]

Additional complaints against inadequate sanitation, food and lodgings contributed to the United States-Mexican labor suspension. Intensive United States pacification efforts were conducted in order to satisfy Mexican grievances and end the abrogation of the 1943 non-farm labor binational agreement. William G. Maclean of the Department of State and Arthur W. Motley, Chief of the Employment Office of the Bureau of Placement, WMC, arrived in Mexico City to end the railroad labor program impasse. They personally delivered an urgent telegram from

Brigadier General C. D. Young, Deputy Director of ODT to Ambassador Messersmith.[101] Joseph Eastman wired Messersmith that the bracero pact suspension was
injurious to United States security because of the "urgent need for additional
railroad labor in (the) war effort."[102] In October, 1943, Eastman requested
Undersecretary of State Edward R. Stettinius to "forcibly" communicate the
necessity of reestablishing the Mexican national importation program.[103] Mexico's
refusal to export Mexican railroad labor from late summer to late fall, 1943,
reflected its true misgivings over United States treatment of the braceros.
Mexico's propensity to suspend agreements became evident throughout the farm labor
program as well and reflected the ongoing diplomatic tension and disagreement
between both nations.

Another problem which contributed to Mexican workers' dissatisfaction
was hazardous work. The United States usually through the WMC Mexican representative notified the Mexican Ministry of Labor when death occurred.[104] Antonio
Reyes Medina, an employee for the Southern Pacific, died from being struck by a
train near Bishop, California, on July 12, 1945.[105] Apolonio Ruiz Gonzales was
killed in the same manner near Echota, New York, while working for the New York
Central.[106] The causes for those bracero deaths were varied. One was the
inability to adapt to a new environmental climate coupled with the railroads'
crude responses to heat prostration. Ismael Aldana Sanchez died of heat prostration on July 30, 1945, in Barstow, California, while working for the New
York, New Haven and Hartford. Mariano Hernandez Carreno was assigned to the
Southern Pacific and died as a result of sunstroke in Arizona on July 17, 1944.
Several deaths were not work-related. Among these were tuberculosis, meningitis,
heart disease, automobile accidents, and tooth infections, apoplectic convulsions
and appendicitis. Other deaths were macaberesque. Andres Hernandez Deave hanged
himself in jail in Nevada. Two other employees for the Southern Pacific, Pedro
Jaramillo Vargas and Lopez Artega, died in separate knifing brawls on July 24, 1944,
and July 31, 1945, respectively. Most braceros, however, were unprepared for
physically oppressive work. The profile of the Mexican worker was described in
one WMC inspection tour as being "better educated and more citified" than domestic
track laborers.[107] Most of them were unskilled rural workers who simply could
not adapt to the physical rigors of maintenance-of-way labor. The work was danger-
ous with scores of Mexicans paying for it with their lives.

Many workers claimed they were denied pay. Several workers demanded
back pay from a few days to several months. Again, the New York Central was a
major target for braceros, who alleged that they were not compensated for work
performed.[108] Another problem was accounting for the lost or missing Mexican
railroad worker. It was commonplace for anxious mothers who had not received
letters from their sons in the United States to contact the WMC. The Commission
in turn would dutifully attempt to locate the missing son and was successful in
many cases. The Burlington Railroad reported a total of 141 missing during its
participation in the program, from December 10, 1943, to January 17, 1946.[109]

The unions wanted domestic labor to be used exclusively and were
vituperatively critical of the railroad bracero program. The unions were unsuccessful in their attempts at influencing the program. They criticized but
rarely controlled. The domestic railroad wage rate was only a paltry fifty-seven
cents an hour in 1946. Railroad unions failed to force a withholding tax upon

the Mexican to reduce his take-home pay. Union anger mounted when they charged that Mexican living conditions were superior to those that domestic workers received. Yet, they were unable to obtain work provision guarantees for their own workers while the United States-Mexican agreement guaranteed them for Mexicans.[110] In retrospect, the unions articulated many justifiable complaints. The two major ones were that railroads with implicit government approval forced the importation of alien labor by offering wages domestic labor could not accept and were responsible in large part for procrastinating total repatriation until a year after the Second World War had ended. From the union standpoint, the non-farm bracero program ignored the needs of domestic labor by producing a cheap foreign labor supply for the railroads.

The railroad bracero program demonstrated both the "push" factors of an underdeveloped Mexican economy and the "pull" factors of a railroad industry hungry for cheap labor. Because of the rigorous work involved and the culture shock which many braceros experienced, the desperate economic situation in Mexico was predominant in compelling them to volunteer to become abused strangers in a foreign land.

Footnotes:

1. Robert C. Jones, Mexican War Workers in the United States: The Mexico-United States Manpower Recruiting Program and Its Operation (Washington: Pan American Union, 1945), p. 26.

2. Ibid.

3. Cited from Mexican Folder, July 9, 1942, Rural Industries Division, Bureau of Placement, War Manpower Commission (RG 211), National Archives.

4. Untitled Report by the Rural Industries and Migratory Labor Section, undated, Mexican Truck Labor Folder, Office of Operations, United States Employment Service, Foreign Labor Section, Bureau of Placement, War Manpower Commission, NA. (Hereafter USES Report.)

5. Jones, War Workers, p. 27.

6. USES Report, p. 2

7. 57 Stat. 1353. George S. Messersmith, United States Ambassador to Mexico and Esequial Padilla, Mexican Foreign Affairs Minister, were the individuals who exchanged the notes.

8. USES Report, p. 3.

9. 57 Stat. 1353-1358

10. It should be pointed out that the April, 1943, agreement does not delineate particular types of Mexican work. The word "railroad" does not appear. The agreement specifies non-agricultural labor which obviates the creation of a different agreement for every occupation which hired Mexicans. Mexican non-agricultural labor worked almost exclusively on the railroad, however, with exceptions discussed below.

11. Memorandum, William G. MacLean to State Department, April 16, 1943, Authorizations and Procedures, WMC (RG 211), NA

12. 57 Stat. 1355. The agreement here is vague. Changes in occupation can be either by inter-industrial change, i.e., from a railroad to a mining occupation, or intra-industrial, i.e. from a maintenance-of-way man to a railroad electrician. As seen below, this vagueness created confusion as to the legality of work transfers and upgraded work so that further regulations and directives were essential.

13. Albert L. Nickerson, Director, Bureau of Placement, to Regional Directors, July 1, 1943. Mexican Track Labor Program, 1943-46, Folder WMC (RG 211), NA. If there was non-compliance, WMC could direct employer to remedy employment conditions. Should non-compliance continue, worker(s) were to be removed and repatriated at expense of deviant employer. (Hereafter: Nickerson Regulations.)

14. MacLean Memorandum. The wording of the August 4, 1942, Agreement with regard to implement purchasing read: "The Mexican Government through the Banco de Credito Agricola will take care of the security of the savings of the workers to be used for payment of the agricultural implements, which may be made available to the Banco de Credito Agricola in accordance with exportation permits for shipment to Mexico with the understanding that the Farm Security Administration will recommend priority treatment for such implements." The proposed wording in the non-agricultural agreement which was stricken out by the State Department was: "The Mexican Government, through the Banco Nacional de Credito Agricola, will safeguard the security of the workers' savings in order that they may be invested in acquiring agricultural implements; and on its part the Government of the United States of North America will grant export permits and priorities for agricultural implements in an amount equal to the total of the workers' savings fund. These implements will be forwarded to the Government of Mexico, which will arrange their delivery to the returning workers, in accordance with the amount accruing to them from the workers' fund, or the delivery of a cash payment, at the option of the worker."

15. Ibid.

16. 39 Stat. 875.

17. It is probabe that the agreement's vagueness with regard to specifying allowable occupations permitted greater arbitrariness on the part of the Justice Department in deciding the worker's occupation. Eventually, the WMC decided who would work where. See below.

18. John D. Coates to H. L. Carter, May 1, 1945, Bureau of Placement, Records of the Labor Recruitment and Transportation Section, RRB 1945 Folder, War Manpower Commission (RG211), National Archives; Nickerson Regulation. Initially all Mexicans received food stamps. In August 15, 1944, shoe stamps were also issued. After May, 1945, rationing of food and shoes was sharply curtailed, with only twelve railroad lines still issuing food stamps.

19. Cordell Hull to Samuel Hough, December 24, 1943; March 19, 1944; March 25, 1944, Certifications Folder, Bureau of Placement, Foreign Labor Section, War Manpower Commission (RG 211), National Archives; USES Report, p. 4.

20. "Relation of Western Railroad Problem to Placement and Control of Manpower" (undated), "Western Railroads; Employment of Mexican Nationals", Folder: Transport Personnel, Office of Defense Transportation (RG 219), NA.

21. Jones, War Workers, p. 26; USES Report, p. 4.

22. USES Report, p. 4.

23. Preliminary Draft: "A Short History of the War Manpower Commission", June 1948, Goodwin Papers, Truman Library (hereafter Goodwin Draft). In addition to Mexican labor, between 8,500 and 10,000 Canadians worked in lumber camps in New York, Maine, Vermont and New Hampshire. Twenty thousand Jamaicans, Barbadians and

other West Indians were recruited for work in foundries and steel mills while recruitment plans were made to place Puerto Ricans in American defense plants. See also, Report, Whom Shall We Welcome, President's Commission on Immigration and Naturalization, 1953, Records of the President's Commission on Immigration and Naturalization. Truman Library.

24. USES Report, Foreword.

25. WMC Regulation No. 6, 8 F. R. 8592 (Washington), June 17, 1943.

26. Lawrence A. Appley to Murray W. Latimer, May 9, 1943, WMC Authorizations and Procedures Folder, WMC (RG 211), NA.

27. Ibid.

28. Arthur W. Motley to Lawrence I. Hewes, May 5, 1943, WMC Authorizations and Procedures Folder, WMC (RG 211), NA.

29. Appley to Latimer; USES Report, p. 5.

30. For Railroad Retirement Board duties, see: Arthur W. Motley, "Mexico Helps War Effort of Our Railroads", U. S. War Manpower Commission, Manpower Review, December, 1943, p. 2; "Mexicans Mitigate Labor Scarcity", Railway Age, June 10, 1944, p. 1113; WMC Regulation No. 6; Nickerson Regulations; Jones, War Workers, pp. 27-28; Appley to Latimer; USES Report, pp. 6-7.

31. Nickerson Regulations. The first recruiting center for railroad workers was in Mexico City. It eventually was transferred to San Luis Potosi in April, 1944, and then to Queretaro.

32. USES Report, p. 7.

33. Ibid., p. 8

34. "Rules for Admission of Mexican Workers as Railroad Track Laborers", Monthly Labor Review, August, 1943, p. 240.

35. Statement, George E. McNulty to Commission, August 18, 1950, Proceedings at Fort Collins, Colorado, August 18, 1950, Records of the President's Commission on Migratory Labor, Truman Library (hereafter McNulty Statement).

36. Elmer E. Milliman to Lewis B. Schwellenbach, October 23, 1945, Office of War Mobilization and Reconversion Folder. Office of the Secretary, Department of Labor (RG 174), NA. Wage rate was 57¢ an hour. Some had to work 60 hours before getting overtime pay of time and a half.

37. Latimer to Leo E. Keller, October 19, 1945, OWMR Folder, Office of the Secretary, Department of Labor (RG 174), NA.

38. Ibid.

39. Statement, T. C. Carroll, October 17, 1950, West Palm Beach, Florida, October 16-17, Records of the President's Commission on Migratory Labor, Truman Library. (Hereafter referred to as Carroll Statement.)

40. WMC Reg. No. 6, Sec. 909.2(b), 8593.

41. Railway Age, p. 1113

42. Ibid., p. 1114

43. Ibid.; Nickerson Regulations; WMC Reg. No. 6, Sec. 909.2(a), 8593. There was much disputation over the bond from agricultural employers who wanted to be reimbursed if a Mexican "skipped" work and could not be located. Such widespread complaints were not in evidence in the railroad labor program.

44. Railway Age, pp. 1114-15.

45. Ibid., p. 1115.

46. H. L. Carter to WMC Regional Directors, August 28, 1943, Material Submitted by R.R.B. Folder, Records of the Labor Recruitment and Transportation Section, Bureau of Placement, WMC (RG 211), NA; Monthly Labor Review, 240-241; Nickerson Regulations; Jones, War Workers, 34-36.

47. Jones, War Workers, p. 36.

48. Nickerson Regulations.

49. L. Valdez to Harry F. Brown, May 12, 1943, WMC (RG 211), NA.

50. Fact sheet, undated, R.R. Recruiting Drive Folder, Office of Defense Transportation (RG 211), NA.

51. Motley, "Mexico Helps", p. 50.

52. Release: Office of War Information, Manpower Administration (Foreigners) Folder, WMC (RG 211), NA.

53. Release: Office of War Information.

54. Despatch No. 3675, Department of State to the American Ambassador, July 7, 1943, Office File of WMC Representative in Mexico, Foreign Labor Section, Bureau of Placement, WMC (RG 211), NA.

55. Carroll Statement; Telegram, Cordell Hull to Hough, March 19, 1944. Hull ordered that 850 braceros be released to the Baltimore and Ohio for employment in New York, Pennsylvania, Delaware, Maryland, Ohio and Indiana and 275 for the New York, New Haven and Hartford.

56. Report, Contained with RRB, Personnel Needs and Surpluses in the Railroad Industry, June 1, 1944 WMC (RG 211), NA. In addition to those previously named other railroads using Mexican labor were: Baltimore and Ohio, Boston and Maine; Chicago and Northwestern; Chicago, Burlington and Quincy; Chicago, Milwaukee, St. Paul and Pacific; Chicago River and Indiana; Delaware, Lackawanna and Western; Erie; Florida East Coast; Forth Worth and Denver City; Great Northern; Indiana Harbor Belt; Lehigh Valley; Long Island; New York Central; New York, Chicago and St. Louis; New York, New Haven and Hartford; Northern Pacific; Pacific Fruit Express; Panhandle and Santa Fe; and the Pennsylvania Railroad.

57. Business Week, October 14, 1944, p. 54. Mexican labor accounted for 72% of the Southern Pacific's track labor--8,325 out of 11,560. The Southern Pacific, the first company to employ Mexican railroad labor, claimed a 185% freight hauling increase from 1939 to 1944 and a 403% passenger increase rate in the year 1944 using 1941 as a comparable period.

58. Jones, War Workers, p. 40.

59. USES Report, p. 9. Other figures were: 135,283 and "over 136,000". See respectively, Whom Shall We Welcome and Goodwin Draft.

60. "List of the 32 Railroads Now Employing Mexican Nationals", Mexican Folder, WMC (RG 211), NA; USES Report, p. 9. Besides those listed above, others using foreign Mexican contracted labor were the Colorado and Southern Railway Company; Gulf, Colorado and Santa Fe Railway Company; Maine Central Railroad and Portland Terminal Companies. By March, 1945, five railroads were pending for receiving labor. Since the total number of railroads increased from 32 to 35, some of the following were granted workers with one refusing the allotment given to it: Chicago, St. Paul, Minneapolis and Omaha; Illinois Central System; Missouri Pacific; and Pere Marquette and Reading Company.

61. USES Report, p. 13.

62. Ibid., p. 14.

63. Churchill Murray to Sidney O'Donoghue, August 30, 1945; Daily File, 1945 Folder, Office Files of the WMC Representative in Mexico, Foreign Labor Section, Bureau of Placement, WMC (RG 211), NA.

64. A. E. Lyon to Secretary Schwellenbach, October 24, 1945, OWMR Folder, Office of the Secretary, Department of Labor (RG 174), NA.

65. Carroll Statement.

66. Ibid.

67. John W. Snyder to Schwellenbach, November 1, 1945, OWMR Folder, Office of the Secretary, Department of Labor (RG 174), NA.

68. Ibid.

69. USES Report. p. 13.

70. Memorandum, J. Bradley Haight to John D. Coates, June 9, 1945, Foreign Workers Files Folder, Bureau of Placement, Records of the Labor Recruitment and Transportation Section, War Manpower Commission (RG 211), NA.

71. USES Report, p. 13.

72. Latimer to Milliman, October 22, 1945, OWMR Folder, Office of the Secretary, Department of Labor (RG 174). NA.

73. H. G. Carter to Landon, August 18, 1945; October 10, 1945, RRB, 1944 and 1945 Folder, Bureau of Placement, Records of the Labor Recruitment and Transportation Section, War Manpower Commission (RG 211), NA.

74. Latimer to Milliman, October 22, 1945.

75. Ibid.

76. Memorandum No. 3183, State Department, October 19, 1944, Daily File, 1944 Folder, WMC (RG 211), NA.

77. Ibid.

78. Schwellenbach to Lyon, March 27, 1946, Mexican Folder, Office of the Secretary, Department of Labor (RG 174), NA.

79. "Railroad's Burden", Business Week, January 1, 1944, p. 44.

80. Milliman to Schwellenbach, October 23, 1945.

81. Joseph B. Eastman to Edward R. Stettinius, October 13, 1943, Mexican Labor Folder, Deputy Director, Office of Defense Transportation (RG 211), NA.

82. Memorandum, H. L. Carter to Washington Representative, September 2, 1943, Material Submitted by RRB Folder, Records of the Labor Recruitment and Transportation Section, Bureau of Placement, WMC (RG 211), NA.

83. Ibid.

84. Excerpt from W. J. Macklin to W. H. Kirkbride, July 12, 1943, Material Submitted by RRB Folder. Records of the Labor Recruitment and Transportation Section, Bureau of Placement, WMC (RG 211), NA.

85. Excerpts from Minutes of Meeting of Committee on Mexican Importation Program, August 28, 1943, Material Submitted by RRB Folder, Records of the Labor Recruitment and Transportation Section, Bureau of Placement, WMC (RG 211), NA.

86. Churchill Murray to John D. Coates, November 17, 1944, Delegations of Authority Folder, Office Files of the WMC Representative in Mexico, Foreign Labor Section, Bureau of Placement, WMC (RG 211), NA. For additional bracero complaints against NYC food in Michigan see: Memorandum, Coates to Murray,

July 9, 1945, New York Central Folder, Bureau of Placement, Chief Foreign Labor Section, WMC (RG 211). NA.

87. McNulty Statement.

88. Jones, War Workers, p. 37.

89. Minutes of Mexican Importation Program.

90. Carter to Washington Representative, September 2, 1943.

91. Eastman to Stettinius, October 13, 1943.

92. USES Report, p. 10.

93. WMC No. 6, Sec. 909.9, 8594.

94. Goodwin Draft; Railway Age, 1112-1113; Jones, War Workers, pp. 32-33. At no time was non-agricultural labor allowed to perform agricultural labor although miscreants were found.

95. Eastman to Stettinius, October 13, 1943.

96. Airgrams, George Messersmith to Cordell Hull, November 30, 1942; December 14, 1942; December 15, 1942; Foreigners and POWs Folder. Reports and Analysis Service Historical Section, War Manpower Commission (RG 211), NA. Ten months before the program, the Vivianna Mining Company of Alpine, Texas, had unsuccessfully requested fifty Mexicans.

97. Samuel B. Hough to Motley, July 2, 1943, Office Files of the WMC Representative in Mexico, Foreign Labor Section, WMC (RG 211), NA.; Nickerson Regulations. During the program there were requests for Mexicans to work in rubber companies, packing industries (Swift, Armour, Cudahy), steel mills and sawmills. Those who did work in these occupations were either wetbacks or others who surreptitiously broke their contracts with other employers, namely farm or railroad. See John R. McCusker to Robert Clarke, October 13, 1943, Rural Industries Division, Bureau of Placement, WMC (RG 211), NA.

98. Macklin to Director of Employment and Claims, December 24, 1943, RRB-1944 Folder, Records of the Labor Recruitment and Transportation Section, Bureau of Placement, WMC (RG 211), NA.

99. Ibid.

100. Quoted from Memorandum, Charles L. Hodge to Robert L. Clark, January 4, 1944, RRB Folder, Records of the Labor Recruitment and Transportation Section, Bureau of Placement, WMC (RG 211), NA.

101. General C. D. Young to MacL-an, August 31, 1943, Mexican Labor Folder, Office of Defense Transportation (RG 219), NA; Percy L. Douglas to General Young, August 28, 1943, Mexican Labor Folder, Deputy Director, ODT (RG 219), NA.

102. Telegram, Eastman to George Messersmith, undated, Mexican Labor Folder, Deputy Director, ODT (RG 219), NA.

103. Eastman to Stettinius, October 13, 1943.

104. Churchill Murray to Luis Fernandez del Campo, 1944-1945, Certifications Folder, Bureau of Placement, Foreign Labor Section, War Manpower Commission (RB 211), NA. There can be found scattered chaotically in the WMC files dozens of 3 by 5 cards which contain information concerning deaths, sickness, denials of pay, whereabouts, and extensions of leave.

105. Certification of a multitude of deaths occurring on the Southern Pacific may be found in: Telegrams, Samuel B. Hough to the Secretaria del Trabajado y Provision Social; Churchill Murray to the Secretaria del Trabajado y Provision Social; Walter J. Macklin to the Secretaria del Trabajado y Provision Social, Southern Pacific Deaths Folder, War Manpower Commission (RG 211), NA.

106. Dozens of braceros died while working for the New York Central; New York Central and New York, Chicago and Saint Louis Deaths Folder, War Manpower Commission (RG 211), National Archives.

107. Carter to Regional Directors, August 28, 1943, Material Submitted to RRB Folder, Records of the Labor Recruitment and Transportation Section, WMC (RG 211), NA.

108. Coates to Murray, New York Central Folder, War Manpower Commission (RG 211), National Archives.

109. McNulty Statement.

110. Carroll Statement; McNulty Statement.

CHAPTER IV

BLACKLISTS AND BINATIONAL TENSIONS, 1943-1947

In March, 1943, the War Food Administration replaced the Farm
Security Administration as the principal government agency in charge of the
Mexican farm labor program. The wartime phase of the binational migratory
labor program ended in April, 1947, with the passage of Public Law 40 providing
for the repatriation of all foreign workers by December, 1947. This law also
placed the authority for recruitment and placement in the United States Employment Service. The War Food Administration of the Department of Agriculture
was responsible for the program from April, 1943, until its abolition in June,
1945, when the Department of Agriculture assumed command until January, 1948.
Colonel Philip G. Bruton, on loan from the War Department, was director of
interstate and foreign labor.[1]

The four-year period from April, 1943 to April, 1947, witnessed the
intensification of diplomatic tension dealing with the treatment of Mexican imported labor and the rapidly emerging problem of the wetback. Mexicans began
to penetrate all regions of the United States. Depending on one's point of view,
the acceleration of recruitment with the subsequent geographical expansion of
the program resulted in a national problem or an expanded Mexican contribution
to the allied war effort. Another emerging highlight of this period was a
developing Congressional preoccupation with the program which manifested itself
in a spate of legislation dealing with appropriation, continuation and eventually abolition of the wartime binational labor program.

There was an abundance of congressional legislation dealing with the
Mexican-United States farm labor program from April 1943 to April 1947. Public
Law 217 which was passed on December 23, 1943, extended the Farm Labor Supply
Program from December 31, 1943, to January 31, 1944.[2] For the remainder of 1944,
the Farm Labor Supply Appropriation Act of 1944 (Public Law 229, February 14, 1944)
appropriated $30,000,000 to the War Food Administration to maintain an adequate
supply of farm workers. The War Food Administration was authorized to "cooperate
with the Secretary of State in the negotiation and renegotiation of agreements
with foreign governments relating to the importation of workers into the United
States."[3] The act provided for easy recruitment of foreign workers by waiving requirements compelling each worker to provide documentary evidence of his country
of birth and to pay a head tax. The Farm Labor Supply Appropriation Act of 1944
continued policies established in Public Law 45 (April 29, 1943) which placed impedi-
ments upon the hiring of domestic migrants to insure a large continuous supply of
foreign labor. Section 4(a) made it difficult to transport intrastate workers to
locations of inadequate farm employment. In addition, domestic farm workers were
not guaranteed a minimum wage, adequate housing, a forty-hour work week, the rights
of collective bargaining or union membership. The funds of both Public Law 45 and
the Farm Labor Supply Act, 1944 (Public Law 229) could be spent only to secure the

above rights for foreign labor covered by international agreement.[4] The provisions of this Farm Labor Supply Appropriation Act were of basic importance
throughout the Mexican wartime labor supply program.

Congress continued to appropriate funds for the foreign labor importa-
tion program in 1945 with the First Supplemental Appropriation Act, 1945 (Public
Law 529, December 22, 1944). This act continued the authority and funding of
Public Law 229 through December 31, 1945, and appropriated an additional
$20,000,000.[5]

The First Deficiency Appropriation Act, 1946 (Public Law 269, December 28, 1945) also sustained the Farm Labor Supply Appropriation Act, 1944 (Public
Law 229) through December 31, 1946.[6] This bill is of great importance, for it represented the initial postwar Congressional attempt to prolong the labor program.
The original justification for this binational labor program, it will be recalled,
had been that the United States had lost a major segment of its agricultural work
force to the armed forces, necessitating foreign labor as an emergency replacement.
Even though World War II ended four months before its passage, Public Law 269
<u>increased</u> the Congressional appropriation from $20,000,000 for 1945 to $25,000,000
for 1946. The rationale for the increase was to maintain "the orderly transition
from war to peace". Actually, Congress was eager to continue providing a cheap
supply of foreign labor at the expense of hiring more costly domestic labor.
Congress felt that the possibility of a food shortage waa strong and was prepared
to be criticized for spending too much in importing foreign labor rather than
having too little food. Congressional debate reveals no inclination to end the
act was written that should there be any "official determination of the cessation
of hostilities", this would not effect the continued importation of Mexican labor.

Unlike the railroad component of imported labor, there was no immediate
postwar effort to repatriate Mexican agricultural labor and terminate the program.
Congress' first postwar act dealing with foreign labor increased its appropriation;
it loosely interpreted the requirements of reconverting to peacetime domestic labor
and served notice to many critics of the program that a wartime emergency measure
would be perpetuated indefinitely into the postwar era.

The program was extended through June 30, 1946, with the Third Deficiency
Appropriation Act of 1946 (Public Law 521, July 23, 1946).[8] It appropriated an ad-
ditional twelve million and extended the authority of the important Farm Labor Supply
Appropriation Act of 1944 through June 1947.

Public Law 707 became law on August 9, 1946, and solidified Congressional
determination to stay the foreign labor market. This act has been called the
"first legislative authorization of the program. It approved action which had already been taken on such a basis that removal of war authority could not affect its
legality."[10]

Before workers were imported into the United States, each prospective
employer filed an application entitled "The Application for Permission to Retain
and/or Import Mexican Agricultural Labor" with the Immigration and Naturalization
Service stating that if domestic labor became available, the employer would dismiss

foreign Mexican labor and agree to terminate the Individual Work Contract which he signed with each laborer. Upon receiving Mexican nationals, the employer signed "The Memorandum of Understanding as to the Duration of Employment of Foreign Labor in American Agriculture".[11] This memorandum reaffirmed the right of the United States Employment Service or other appropriate agency to replace Mexican labor when domestic labor became available. It is not surprising, given Section 4(a) of both Public Law 45 and Public Law 229 and the organized power of farm groups that no contract workers were ever repatriated to Mexico as a result of domestic labor replacement.[12]

The agency in charge of the recruitment process was the Office of Labor of the War Food Administration which was initially established in March, 1943. Before farm workers reached their destination in the United States, the Office of Labor secured appropriate transportation to the United States, temporary housing before arrival at work destination and food en route with the employer bearing the cost. In Mexico, each potential recruit was examined by the United States Public Health Service and by Mexican Public Health Authorities.[13] Mexico had the power to determine ultimately which workers and how many would emigrate.[14]

Farm workers entered the United States under six-month contracts which were renewable upon the consent of worker, employer and both nations. The Mexican national and the War Food Administration were parties to each contract. The recruitment system included the (a) intergovernmental agreement between the United States and Mexico; (b) the contracts of individual workers with the War Food Administration; and (c) the contracts for groups of workers made by individual farmers or grower associations with the War Food Administration.[15]

Foreign migrant labor had to fill out numerous questionnaires, submit to medical examinations, fingerprinting, and sign numerous papers. Part of their medicinal preparation for travel abroad consisted of a compulsory bath and haircut. This regimentation persisted on the train trip northward; each Mexican farm worker received a number, was assigned a seat, and was instructed not to leave the train before it reached its final destination. Even their meals were conducted with military regimen: "In a deep and orderly silence they were taken to the dining-cars, where colored waiters in spotless uniforms served them a meal which they ate without saying a word."[16]

It is important to investigate the profile of the Mexican worker. This study is historical rather than sociological, yet it is based upon Mexican labor, which is a human commodity. The Mexican nationals were exclusively male and generally between twenty and thirty years of age.[17] The majority of them were peasants and unskilled laborers with a few being factory workers and small merchants. They were poor, came from a bucolic background and streamed from their rustic villages in search of employment and fortune in the United States. The latter generally consisted of an hourly wage between ten and sixty-five cents and hour. In spite of their poverty, they were adequately clothed and could be seen wearing sombreros and serapes under their overcoats.[18]

Mexican nationalists were opposed to the manpower drain of thousands of young, mature and strong workers to the United States. Ernesto Lopez Malo, of the National School of Economics in Mexico, bemoaned even the temporary migration of these contract workers, for "they formed a very valuable part of the demographic wealth of Mexico."[19]

During 1943, 52,131 workers were transported to the United States. Before WFA replaced the Farm Security Administration in April 1943, the latter had recruited 11,047 workers whereas the former would recruit 41,084. Mexico continuously erected quotas which represented the maximum number of workers allowed in the United States at one time. In 1943 Mexico increased the quota from 50,000 to 70,000, yet rarely was the quota met.[20] The United States Embassy pressured the Department of State to import more workers in order to convince Mexico that the bracero program was a necessity. The United States requested from Mexico in August, 1943, that the quota be increased to 75,000, notwithstanding the fact that only 40,374 workers had been brought to this country by the end of August. On December 31, 1943, there were 17,000 workers in the United States--58,000 under the amount allowed by the quota.[21] Those Mexicans who did enter in 1943 were credited with saving twenty-one per cent of the California crop.[22] In late November, 1943, Harry F. Brown, a representative of the War Food Administration, announced from Mexico City that he had secured an agreement between Mexico and the United States for the additional importation of 75,000 migrants for fifteen states in the west and southwest for 1944.[23]

The second full year of wartime recruitment continued to fall short of the quota. As was customary, however, the War Food Administration extravagantly claimed that 75,000 Mexican workers were needed to produce farm products in 1944. Mexico even consented to nationwide recruitment outside Mexico City in Irapuato in the state of Guanajuato and Guadalajara in the state of Jalisco. Even the June, 1944, quota was raised from 14,000 to 20,000. In spite of large quotas and the opening of the interior to direct recruiting, the Office of Labor was unable to recruit 75,000 workers.[24] The Mexican Secretariat of Foreign Affairs reported in January, 1944, that 90,000 Mexicans could go to the United States but "the Mexicans now working in the United States are considerably fewer than the number authorized by our government."[25] It is fair to question the motives behind this wartime labor program. In the first two years of its existence, the United States did not recruit the maximum number allowed; the fault lay neither with Mexican intransigence--for the quotas were frequently raised--nor with a lack of foreign workers, since the recruitment process was characterized by a glut in the National Stadium in Mexico City with migrants clamoring for emigration. The lack of a maximum recruiting effort can be explained in part by wetback traffic, which obviated farmer requests for contract labor and by exaggerated claims of needed Mexican workers.

The intrusion of the wetback as a diplomatic problem begain in 1944. The first of a series of binational meetings to explore directly illegal Mexican labor began on May 30, 1944, at the Foreign Office in Mexico City. Although there were 60,000 contract farm workers in the United States, it was feared that clandestine immigration could undermine the bracero program by undercutting the internationally guaranteed wage rate and forcing more expensive labor to move elsewhere. Among United States delegates attending these anti-wetback diplomatic negotiations were George S. Messersmith, Ambassador to Mexico; Earl G. Harrison, Commissioner of Immigration and Naturalization; and Howard K. Travera, head of the visa division in the State Department.[26]

In June 1944 The Mexican Secretary of Labor Statistics announced a quota which called for enlisting 75,000 farm workers for 1945, with 48,000 arriving by June 1945.[27] In spite of reports that the program might possibly be phased out after V-J Day, the Mexican Ministry of Foreign Relations affirmed the 75,000 farm worker quota in late 1944.[28] Again the quota of 75,000 was not attained; only 49,457 Mexican contract laborers migrated to the United States in 1945.

During 1946, 32,406 Mexican farm workers were recruited and transported to the United States, with the first 818 of them leaving Irapuato, Mexico, on April 17, 1946. Despite President Truman's proclamation on December 31, 1946, ending the state of hostilities which would affect the laws under which Mexicans would be brought in, the Department of Agriculture immediately solicited Congress to extend the legal waiver on immigration requirements in order to satisfy an alleged urgent labor shortage in sugar beet and general farm industries.[29] In all, the United States recruited 309,538 workers from September 1942 to December 1947. This recruitment process, from 1943-1947, was marred by Mexican protestations of discrimination and threats to abandon the importation program. Inevitably, an American deputation would scurry down to Mexico City to pacify the disgruntled Mexican Government to continue the bracero program and allow nationwide placement throughout the United States. It was the Texas problem which created the greatest amount of international acrimony during this period.

Texas was considered the most repressive state in which a Mexican national could reside. Although discrimination against Mexican nationals was widespread in the United States, nowhere was it so severe or blatant as in Texas. In regions, such as Texas, where slavery existed up to the second half of the nineteenth century, non-whites were considered inferior to whites. Many of the braceros were a mixture of Indian and Spanish and were discriminated against because of their lack of racial purity. The repercussions detracted from relations between Mexico and the United States.

The Mexican daily Excelsior editorialized that Mexico "will defend the rights and the human status of Mexicans who reside in a country which is fighting to preserve the principles of democracy and equality in the world."[30]

Mexico expressed its anxiety over discrimination in Texas by blacklisting the state as unfit for Mexican labor. The input for this drastic decision in June and July, 1943, were varied. Domestic political considerations were just as responsible for the ban as were humanitarian considerations for the workers. Various Mexican union, agricultural and anti-government groups opposed the bracero program as excessive acquiescence to United States wartime needs. Although the nationalistic fervor of President Lazaro Cárdenas was no longer institutionalized, the government was still sensitive to organized criticism that accused the administration of sacrificing nationalism in order to satisfy United States domestic requirements.[31]

The Texas blacklisting also resulted from a United States-authorized sponsoring of a May, 1943, invasion in which thousands of wetback Mexicans entered Texas under the provisions of Section 5(g) of Public Law 45. This action ignored the international provisions of the program as established in April 1943 and precipitated Mexican reprisals. If the United States could be goaded into subverting

Mexican participation in the program by Texas farmers who wanted cheap labor without acknowledging the binational work guarantees, Mexico would simply stop the flow of legally contracted labor.

The principal reason, however, for refusing to send contract labor to Texas during this period was Texan prejudice against Mexicans. Throughout the Second World War, Texas Governor Coke Stevenson beseeched Mexican Foreign Labor Minister Ezequiel Padilla to permit the flow of recruited labor to Texas. Stevenson created a Texas Good Neighbor Commission in September 1943 and promised that State law officials would deal severely with Texans discriminating against Mexicans. Padilla believed Stevenson's proposals were insufficient and vowed to prevent further emigration to Texas until after the "wave of racial prejudice had subsided."[32]

The Texas problem became insoluble as Texas farmers increasingly used wetback labor to subvert the international conditions of employment. Texas farmers, ranchers, and growers conspired to import illegal non-contract labor. A three-day conference in Mexico City between both nations, from May 29, 1944, to June 2, 1944, produced a United States pledge to beef up its border patrol, remove wetbacks in south Texas, and repatriate any worker at Mexico's request. In spite of this agreement, which tended to reaffirm the official United States position against illegal immigration, persistent reports of discrimination destroyed any Texas settlement.

A product of the racism in Texas was the establishment of the quasi-governmental Comite Mexicano Contra el Rasismo (Mexican Committee Against Racism) in August 1944.[33] Its monthly organ, Fraternidad, cited United States instances of discrimination against Mexicans in education, labor and restaurants. This blue-ribbon liberal committee recommended tough anti-discriminatory legislation as the best short-term device to combat racism in Texas with its total eradication dependent upon "the raising of the cultural level of the population."[34] The Mexican press took up the theme of discrimination in America. Lectura, a Mexican bi-monthly editorialized:

> In the United States, they despise us. They call us greasy
> and dirty and do not consider us worthy to associate with
> them. ...It does not matter to the American that he (the
> Mexican) has money and that he has earned it with the sweat of
> his brow. ...In some places he cannot even shop in the stores.
> ...Racial discrimination ...exists because there are North
> Americans who believe themselves ...superior ... North Ameri-
> cans are waging a war against Germany and against the ideas
> for which Germany is fighting, one of which is the superiority
> of the Aryan. But that group of North Americans who despise
> the Mexican has become seduced by the racial ideas of Germany.
> And above all: the United States, while opposing the racial
> theories of Germany, feeds, sustains and cultivates this racism
> in its own territory against Mexicans and against Negroes.[35]

Ultima Noticias in its May 10, 1945, edition offered this appraisal of United States treatment of Mexican farm labor:

> The North American conscience is against discrimination. The
> neighboring countries of Mexico and the United States should

cooperate so that an end may be put to discrimination, since this discrimination casts aspersions on the prestige of the United States.[38]

The vexing problem of containing illegal Mexican labor from traversing the Mexican-Texas border prompted another meeting between representatives of Mexico and the United States. This time they met in Washington, D.C., and embodied their recommendations in a "Joint Memorandum of Conversation" on January 9, 1945.[37] The recommendations which included increasing border patrol personnel in Texas were never implemented successfully, for the numbers of wetbacks increased dramatically as the 1940s progressed.

Not only did the volume of illegal Mexican labor intensify but also the sordidness of their treatment. Newsweek magazine, in describing illegal Mexican labor as "the very backbone of the prosperity of the ... lower Rio Grande Valley", ran a series of articles describing murder on the Rio Grande.[38] By October 8, 1945, thirty-eight bodies had been found; these wetbacks, men and women, had been murdered by gangs specializing in "human smuggling and wholesale murder". [39] Women were reported to have been mutilated beyond recognition and crucified in efforts to strip them of their earnings as they returned to Mexico. Through October 15, 1945, forty-eight illegals had been murdered.[40] Newsweek charged that United States immigration authorities ignored the wetback invasion because without it, "Bank vaults in the valley towns might not be bulging with farmers' cash."[41]

A dramatic case study of this illegal influx into Texas was made of Hidalgo County, Texas, from whence 14,592 wetbacks were deported between December, 1946 and January, 1947. Eleven per cent were under sixteen and eight per cent were female.[42] This composition of child and woman was of major demographic importance. As previously mentioned, all contracted Mexican labor was male and stayed in the United States for a limited period of time. When the Mexican ban on contract labor in Texas commenced in 1943, illegal labor swarmed across the border with many remaining in Texas and producing families--and important contribution to the present Mexican-American population in the United States.[43]

Another study of a Texas county for the fiscal year 1947-1948 revealed that many had an average income of less than ten dollars per week; almost half earned less than twenty dollars a week and more than eight per cent had an annual average income of less than $2,000.[44] This labor, which was illegal, deportable, and not included under the aegis of international work guarantees, was easily exploited by avaricious Texas farmers at a wage rate of ten to fifteen cents an hour.

Diplomatically, there had been no progress in solving the Texas imbroglio. By 1947, four years after the start of the international worker importation program, there was still no contract labor going from Mexico to Texas and the illegal labor which helped perpetuate the Mexican ban continued at a torrential pace.[45] Not surprisingly, the two nations decided to confer once again over the twin problems of blacklist and wetback in Mexico City between January 27, 1947, and February 4, 1947, with two binational agreements emerging on March 10, 1947.

These agreements supplemented but did not replace the April 1943, Mexican-United States agreement. They legalized wetback labor throughout the United States with one agreement specifically applying to illegals in Texas. Under the agreement, machinery was set up to repatriate them to Mexico, certify them and return them rapidly to the United States. Mexico agreed to establish recruiting stations at Mexicali near the California border and at Ciudad Juarez and Reynosa just south of Texas.[46] Mexico, despite United States initiative, sought this legalization of its citizens hoping such action would limit the recruitment of additional braceros for work in the United States. As the wetback flood intensified, concern over further Mexican manpower depletion did likewise. By permitting wetbacks to return to Mexico and contracts enabling them to re-enter legally into the United States with the attendant guarantees of minimum working and living conditions, Mexico reasoned that potential wetbacks would wait their turn to reap the benefits of contract protection. Another factor in the legalizing of illegal labor was Mexico's undoubted recognition that illegal farm workers, estimated at 119,000 in April, 1947, could never be eliminated completely. Desperate to find some means of protecting its nationals from indiscriminate exploitation, Mexico opted for legalization to protect the wetbacks and compel Southwestern farmers and growers to honor the internationally sanctioned rights of Mexican farm labor.[47] As will be demonstrated later, Mexico miscalculated the effects of wetback legalization, which severely disrupted the entire bracero program.

These laws which legalized wetbacks and were intended to protect them from mistreatment went into effect April 10, 1947. Their effectiveness in legalizing wetbacks was noteworthy. Wetbacks were taken across the border to Mexico, fingerprinted, issued an identification card and given a copy of a work agreement specifying location and conditions of employment. Once legalized, they returned to the United States where the Mexicans would receive a physical examination aimed at finding symptoms of venereal disease and tuberculosis, and a vaccination against small pox. They were fingerprinted again for the Federal Bureau of Investigation, photographed and issued another identification card.[48]

The agreement, which pertained specifically to non-contract labor in Texas, was ineffective in reversing objectionable treatment of Mexican citizens in that State. This supplementary international agreement specified that if a worker labored more than eight hours a day, "the extra hours shall be paid in the manner specified by the laws of the State where the ranch is situated." In Texas, there was no state law providing for overtime pay, which would necessarily result in the farmer paying the guaranteed hourly wage of twenty cents regardless of the number of hours worked. The strongest indictment of this agreement was that neither wetbacks nor contract labor were needed in Texas and should not have been legalized or allowed to work there. Pauline R. Kibbe, executive secretary of the Texas Good Neighbor Commission, wrote that "there is no scarcity of resident labor in the Rio Grande Valley" who would be willing to work for a decent wage.[49] Thousands of unemployed Mexican-Americans who were driven out of Texas by poorly paid Mexican labor dispersed all over the United States in search of work where they would not have to compete with cheap labor.

The Texas affair was certainly the most dramatic and difficult problem during the 1943-1947 period of the alien manpower program. It dramatized the treatment Mexicans received at the hands of American farmers and growers; it demonstrated the seemingly insurmountable problems of containing wetback traffic and the effects wetbacks had upon the domestic agricultural work force. The Texas situation

56

exacerbated diplomatic tensions and triggered the usual strong Mexican response to mistreatment of its citizens. However, the problems of the Mexicans in the United States were not confined to Texas, nor were United States citizens always the per-petrators.

ethnic
succession

A major problem confronting Mexican imported farm workers was housing. In most areas, especially in California, there was a housing shortage. Mexicans slept in quarters previously used to induct Japanese-Americans before the latter were concentrated in permanent barracks. Sometimes Mexican nationals slept in old Army barracks.[50] The Office of Labor of the War Food Administration was charged with the responsibility of enforcing minimum housing standards whether the housing was operated by that agency, State Extension Services, individual growers or grower associations. Lieutenant Colonel Wilson R. Buie, the Director of Labor of the Office of Labor, revealed that inadequate housing and sanitation was threatening the international labor program.

> Foreign governments with whom we have agreements have not been
> satisfied with the housing standards of last year. This became
> very material in our negotiations for additional contracts. Con-
> tracts were negotiated only after virtual guarantees on the part
> of the Director of Labor that housing and sanitation this year
> would be in conformity with minimum standards.[51]

Housing in addition to its physical deficiencies contributed to culture shock and a general psychological disorientation. Individual housing units were rare, with barracks being the usual housing pattern. The housing situation helped create the most difficult adjustment to non-family group living. Feelings of home-sickness were not unlike those a fresh army recruit experienced. For both, the change of environment resulted in a severance of family ties and the unaccustomed exposure to severe regimentation. The Mexican was technically free to abrogate his contract but group and employer pressure restricted him from doing so until his six-month contract expired. Nonetheless, many longed for reunion with their families and the resumption of normal sexual activity. Male-oriented group living increased the propensity for frequenting whore houses when available and nurtured "dreams of how things would be when they went back to Mexico."[52]

Another major irritant to the Mexican was food. Strange food contri-buted to culture shock and was one of the most persistent problems facing the Mexican farm laborer. For the first year after the program began, the Office of Price Administration issued food stamps. Generally, the food was prepared by non-Mexican cooks who did not share the dietetic predilections of the Mexicans; Mexican laborers, who were accustomed to corn meal tortillas, beans and chili, detested the cold sandwich lunch which was their common midday fare. Their tastes were simple but distinctive, and as strangers in a foreign land, they harbored fears and doubts about adapting to a new diet.[53]

The meals cost the worker between thirty-five and fifty cents and either a federal agency or the private employer prepared them. The Shelter and Feeding Division, Operations Branch, Office of Labor, had the responsibility for supervising the entire food operation. It was their stated policy, which was never operation-alized, that the Mexican should receive a diet which was nutritionally adequate and which conformed to their native diet.[54]

Most of the Mexicans brought to the United States as farm workers spoke no English, which further handicapped them in their attempts to cope with a new environment. As was the case with Mexican railroad labor in the United States, their foremen or field supervisors spoke no Spanish, yet demanded immediate compliance to orders. One example of the difficulties caused by language barriers occurred if the laborers were hospitalized, since they were oftentimes unable to communicate the symptoms of their physical problems.[55]

Many Mexican nationals experienced difficulties and abuse before entering the United States. Certain Mexican officials enriched themselves at the expense of the braceros. A major Mexican government scandal erupted in January, 1945, when it was learned that three Mexican Federal Deputies had sold certificates of eligibility to workers in violation of Mexican and international law. Defrauding potential crop pickers or track laborers in the United States resulted in the indictments of Carlos Madrazo, Tellez Vargas, president of the Moving Pictures Workers Union, and Sacramento Joffre. Federal Deputies, who composed the Chamber of Deputies, indicted only with the President's consent. President Manuel Avila Camacho consented to these first indictments of Federal Deputies since the autocracy of Porfirio Díaz in 1907. The president requested that the Chamber of Deputies, which was in recess when the indictments were handed down on January 16, 1947, be convoked into an extraordinary session for the purpose of removing the parliamentary immunity of its indicted members.[56]

On April 28, 1947, the American Congress passed Public Law 40 which was intended to eliminate the foreign labor program. The law stated that the program "may be continued up to and including December 31, 1947, and thereafter shall be liquidated within thirty days."[57] It ended the wartime legislative authority of the Farm Labor Supply Appropriation Act of 1944 (Public Law 229) and permitted Mexican farm laborers to remain in this country only until the abolition of the program. Indeed, many sources view this act as an historic termination of the Mexican wartime farm labor supply program notwithstanding the fact that the program was not abolished but merely altered structurally.[58] *no de facto change*

Immediately upon the passage of Public Law 40, United States agricultural employers, claiming an acute labor shortage, petitioned the Immigration and Naturalization Service to extend the immigration of Mexican farm workers beyond the December, 1947 deadline. Suffice to say, less than two months after the so-called congressional termination of the wartime Mexican farm labor supply program, a new international agreement was promulgated on February 21, 1948, allowing for the continued employment of braceros.[59]

Obviously, given the increasingly troublesome non-contract migration, any United States law that failed to acknowledge the existence of illegals or to penalize farmers who used or concealed them was encouraging a permanent foreign labor force in the United States. Within a few weeks after the passage of Public Law 40, there was a resumption of the migration of legally contracted Mexicans to the United States; it was not surprising, however, that Congress would not even consider the possibility of taking the more drastic step of legislating an end to the awesome spectacle of hundreds of thousands of poverty-ridden wetbacks entering the nation.

During the first year of the program, the executive branch and its agencies directed the foreign labor program. The initial financing came out of the President's Emergency Fund and the authorization was provided by executive-sponsored international agreements. The period of executive dominance was never threatened in terms of administration and policy even though Congress from Public Law 217 (December 23, 1943), to Public Law 40 (April 28, 1947), assumed the responsibility for financing the program. The fact that the executive branch was able to continue the bracero program despite Public Law 40 indicated that the locus of power in managing the bracero program lay with the executive branch. Congress was not represented in the diplomatic aspects of the program; although Congress was becoming more concerned with the alien labor program at this juncture its influence was not great.

The Mexican-United States manpower program from April, 1943, up to the passage of Public Law 40 in April, 1947, was a disharmonious diplomatic venture between Mexico and the United States. The interrelated problems of discrimination and illegal labor resulted in a Mexican ban of the use of its workers in Texas and strident Mexican press criticism of the Mexicans' mistreatment. The wetback phenomenon resulted in several Mexican-United States conferences which failed to deal successfully with the problems.

This period illustrated the intense dedication of the Mexican Government to protecting its citizens abroad. The four-year period presaged future Mexican abrogations of the bracero program and increasingly vituperative criticism of the United States. While a basic harmony existed in Mexican-United States relations, this binational labor program consistently provoked problems which threatened to destroy that amity.

Footnotes:

1. New York Times, May 1, 1943, p. 10 (hereafter referred to as NYT.)

2. "Chronology of Recruitment of Mexican Workers for Agricultural Employment in the United States--1941-1951", Chronological File, January 1,
   1951-June 4, 1951, Records of the President's Commission on Migratory
   Labor, Truman Library.

3. 58 Stat. 11-17.

4. Ibid.,Sec. 4(a) and (b), p. 14.

5. 58 Stat. 863.

6. 59 Stat. 645.

7. Congressional Record, 91, 11190, 12107-12109. Senator Millard Tydings
   championed the idea of increasing appropriations regardless of the availability of domestic labor.

8. 60 Stat. 617.

9. 60 Stat. 969.

10. "Chronology", p. 6.

11. Robert C. Jones, Mexico-United States Agricultural Labor Recruitment Pro-
    gram and its Operation, Staff Study Number 1, December 15, 1950 (revised),
    Staff Studies, November 1950-February 1951 Folder, Records of the Presi-
    dent's Commission on Migratory Labor, Truman Library.

12. Ibid.

13. The actual recruitment through August 1944 took place in the National Stadium
    in Mexico. The location of recruitment centers became a heated issue later
    in the program. Southwestern farmers desired border centers to avoid the
    cost of recruiting from the interior. Mexico, on the other hand, did not
    want northern recruiting centers, fearing excessive depletion of Northern
    Mexican labor. The farmers when frustrated resorted to non-contract labor.

14. Marion Parks, "A New Pattern in International Wartime Collaboration", The
    Department of State Bulletin, August 13, 1944, p. 161.

15. Ibid., p. 162.

16. Marco A. Almazan, "The Mexicans Keep 'Em Rolling", The Inter-American (October
    1945), p. 22.

17. Carey McWilliams, "They Saved the Crops", The Inter-American, 2 (August, 1943)
    p. 13.

18. Almazan, "Keep "Em Rolling", pp. 21-22.

19. Ernesto Lopez Malo, "La Emigracion de Trabajadores Mexicanos", Ciencias Sociales, October 1954, p. 224 (translated by the author).

20. Wayne D. Rasmussen, A History of the Emergency Farm Labor Supply Program 1943-1947 (Washington, 1951), pp. 213-215. Department of State figures for 1943 are 56,301 Mexican agricultural workers who left for the United States. The Mexican Secretaria de Governacion cited 75,923 Mexicans leaving for the United States, of which approximately 25,000 were maintenance-of-way train workers.

21. NYT, February 28, 1944; Rasmussen, History, p. 213.

22. Parks, "A New Pattern", p. 161.

23. NYT, November 17, 1943.

24. Rasmussen, History, p. 217

25. NYT, January 20, 1944.

26. NYT, May 31, 1944, p. 5.

27. NYT, June 22, 1944.

28. NYT, December 9, 1944

29. NYT, January 1, 1947; Rasmussen History, p. 218.

30. Cited in, "A Mexican View of Race Relations", The Inter-American, September 1943, p. 30.

31. Otey M. Scruggs, "Texas and the Bracero Program", Pacific Northwest Review, February 1963, p. 257.

32. "No Mexicans Allowed", The Inter-American, September 1943, p. 81; Scruggs, "Texas", p. 256.

33. Scruggs, "Texas", p. 260.

34. Hensley C. Woodbrige, "Mexico and U. S. Racism: How Mexicans View our Treatment of Minorities", Commonweal, June 22, 1945, pp. 236-237. Members of this committee were Mexican luminaries Enrique Gonzales Martinez, President of the committee and a leading Mexican writer; Jaime Torres Bodet, a Foreign Minister; Gustavo Baz, a cabinet officer; Raul Noriega, editor of El Nacional; and Vincente Lombardo Toledano, the most powerful labor leader in Mexican history. In addition to the above, there were scores of other intellectuals, authors, government officials and leaders.

35. Cited in Woodbridge, "Racism", p. 235. Editorials of December 15, 1944, and January 1, 1945.

36. Ibid.

37. "Chronology", p. 5.

38. Newsweek, October 8, 1945, p. 71; March 11, 1946, pp. 70-71.

39. Ibid., October 8, 1945, p. 71.

40. NYT, October 15, 1945. Federal Judge Manuel Gomez Lomeli of the Mexican Second District held five for trial but had previously released eighteen for lack of incriminating evidence.

41. Newsweek, March 11, 1946, p. 71.

42. Pauline R. Kibbe, "Report to the Members of the Good Neighbor Commission of Texas on Lower Rio Grande Valley Trip, April 17-27, 1947", Migratory Labor 1950 Folder, Department of Labor, Office of the Secretary, Gibson File (RG 174), p. 1, NA. (Hereafter referred to as "Good Neighbor".)

43. Kibbe, "Good Neighbor", p. 2.

44. "The Illegal Entry of Mexicans into the United States". Correspondence 1950 Folder, Department of Labor, Office of the Secretary, Creasy Files (RG 174), pp. 3-4.

45. It should be pointed out that Mexico eventually allowed Mexican Nationals to be transferred to Texas from other parts of the United States. Very few transferred due to the undesirability of working there.

46. NYT, March 26, 1947.

47. George O. Coalson, "Mexican Contract Labor in American Agriculture", Southwestern Social Science Quarterly, 33 (December 1952), pp. 228-238.

48. Kibbe, "Good Neighbor", p. 3.

49. Ibid.

50. Anne Roller Issler, "Good Neighbors Lend a Hand", Survey Graphic, October 1943, pp. 390-391.

51. Rasmussen, History, p. 183.

52. Almazán, "Keep "em Rolling", p. 23; Issler, "Lend a Hand", p. 391. Many were quick to condemn these Mexican braceros as immoral pruveyors of vice and venereal disease, ignoring the situation of family separation and all-male companions, which was responsible for much of the "deviant" social behavior.

53. Parks, "A New Pattern", p. 163; Almazan, "Keep 'Em Rolling", p. 23.

54. Rasmussen, History, pp. 185-187, 197.

55. Ibid., p. 197; Almazán, "Keep 'Em Rolling", p. 36.

56. NYT, January 17, 1945, p. 5; Rasmussen, History, p. 214. Seven others were arrested on the same charge of defrauding workers by illegally selling them certificates to expedite their emigration north.

57. 61 Stat. 55.

58. NYT, March 5, 1947; March 13, 1947; April 9, 1947; Coalson, "Mexican Contract Labor", p. 237; Daniel Goott, "Employment of Foreign Workers in United States Agriculture", Department of State Bulletin, July 11, 1949, p. 43. It should be stressed again that, although this study deals with Mexican foreign labor, there were British West Indian nationals from Jamaica, the Bahamas and Barbados.

59. "Chronology", p. 7; Goott, "Foreign Workers", pp. 44-45.

CHAPTER V

DECLINE AND CRISIS: 1948-1950

Public Law 40 did not end the Mexican farm labor program, for there were continuing pressures to prolong it. During the next three years, 1948-1950, the United States and Mexico signed two agreements and met frequently to discuss the program's problems. However, the United States representative to such discussions no longer was the Department of Agriculture, which had directed the binational labor operation from 1943 to 1947 through various subordinate agencies; it lost its farm placement functions to the Department of Labor and the Federal Security Agency.

The increasingly difficult problem of impeding wetback migration was beginning to seriously undermine the labor program. By 1951, the wetback had all but destroyed it. Although Mexican protests and United States apologies dealt with the unlawful migration, it became apparent the latter nation did not intend to halt the influx of non-contract labor. This period reveals that the United States' decision to ignore Mexican labor demands was as much a product of bureaucratic indecision and disagreement as government intent. Some agencies demonstrated concern over the wetbacks' impact as a disruptive influence creating displacement of United States citizens and diplomatic friction between the two nations. United States interagency conflict developed over the priorities of satisfying agribusiness demands as against maintaining amicable Mexican-United States relations. Another prominent feature of this period was the rising opposition of organized labor to the entire alien labor program.

Shortly after the passage of Public Law 40, attempts were made to continue the recruitment process beyond the terminal date of December 1947. Negotiations between the two countries, which began in the winter of 1947, eventually culminated in a new Mexican-United States agreement on February 21, 1948.

The Labor Department had announced in November that there would be a shortage of domestic agricultural manpower for the 1948 harvest season.[1] On November 10, 1947, the United States Embassy proposed binational conversations to draw up conditions and terms under which Mexican nationals could be employed in agricultural labor in the United States.[2] The result was a joint meeting in El Paso, Texas, from November 20, 1947, to December 2, 1947, to arrive at a satisfactory intergovernmental agreement for the continued temporary recruiting of Mexican farm labor for the United States.[3]

The main points of contention at these negotiations concerned the banning of Mexican Labor from Texas and the establishment of border versus interior recruiting. The United States strenuously advocated admitting farm workers to Texas, reasoning that such an act would replace labor which Texan farmers were employing illegally. Governor Beauford Jester of Texas, as had his predecessor Coke Stevenson, pleaded for the ban's removal and proffered a non-discriminatory plan in which state officials would police communities and investigate employers suspected of discrimination. Mexico responded that only through "prior action" could Texas guarantee proper treatment of Mexican nationals.[4]

Southwestern farmers sought border recruitment to cut down the expense of recruiting Mexicans from the interior, but Mexico rejected it, claiming that unemployment was most severe in the interior and that border recruitment would precipitate a mass exodus from the border towns. Mexico stood firm and the agreement stipulated that the "places of contract in the Republic of Mexico shall be freely determined by the Government of Mexico". [5] The meetings ended on December 2, 1947, without a final agreement, because the Mexican President and Foreign Minister insisted upon direct approval of the drafts before final passage.

During this hiatus between December 2, 1947 and February 17, 1948, when the agreement was signed, several governmental agencies and non-governmental organizations fought for continuation of the Mexican labor supply. Robert C. Goodwin, Director of the United States Employment Service, declared that his agency took over the responsibility for recruiting farm labor at a time when "less labor will be available for agriculture than since the end of the war. The demand for farm labor in 1948 probably will be the greatest in peacetime history."[6] The National Canners Association, which represented food packers, called on the Federal Government to secure foreign farm workers for the harvest of food crops in 1948. NCA adopted a resolution at its forty-first annual convention declaring that there was insufficient manpower available for the harvest of canning crops.[7] The Canners' Vice President, John J. McGovern, forecasted a reduction in canned foods and a curtailment in the overall food supply if foreign labor could not supplement domestic labor.[8]

Between February 9 and February 11, 1948, there was another meeting in Mexico with Maurice L. Stafford, First Secretary of the United States Embassy, and Alfonso Guerra, Official Mayor of the Mexican Ministry for Foreign Relations, representing their two nations. They finalized the work of the El Paso Conference on February 17, 1948, when the agreement was signed; an exchange of notes made the pact operative on February 21, 1948.[9]

This agreement superseded those of April 26, 1943 and March 10, 1947.[10] The wartime agreements provided for continual and close United States supervision of the contract. The United States did the contracting, selecting and transporting of workers as well as ensuring their protection under the agreement. The 1948 agreement, on the other hand, while providing for "intervention by the two governments", ordered the Individual Worker Contracts to be on a worker to employer basis. This time, the employer was not defined as the United States Government but an "owner or operator of an agricultural property". It was understood that:

> Neither the United States Employment Service nor the United
> States Immigration and Naturalization Service would actively
> participate either in the recruitment of workers or in any super-
> vision incident to the negotiation of the individual work agree-
> ment, or assume any responsibility for assuring compliance with
> the terms of the agreement, either on the part of the worker or
> the employer.[11]

Under the agreement United States participation was crisis-oriented except when it provided Mexico with information concerning the general manpower employment situation.

Only those employers who received certification from the USES could contract Mexican nationals. The agreement stated in priciple that Mexican workers in the United States should not suffer any discriminatory acts. Mexican braceros, on the other hand, could not displace domestic labor or lower the prevailing domestic wage rate. In essence, both domestic and foreign worker were to be protected from each other.

Mexico could unilaterally select the location of recruitment centers provided that "they not be south of a line from coast to coast through Guadalajara and Queretaro", which represented a 1,000-mile limit from the border.

Mexican Consuls and USES personnel were authorized to periodically inspect the work camps; however, no positive institutionalized supervision was contemplated, since governmental supervision was applied on an ad hoc basis.

The wetback migration, which the State Department described as "the most formidable problem confronting the United States and Mexican Government in connection with the migratory labor program", finally attained sufficient international recognition to be mentioned in the farm worker agreement.[12] Employers were denied Mexican contract farm workers if they hired wetback labor. For the first time in these binational agreements both nations dedicated themselves to stem the illegal flow of Mexican migratory workers into the United States and to rapidly repatriate those who were apprehended.

The international agreement provided that both nations draw up an Individual Work Contract that would define the relationship between laborer and employer. This contract delineated the terms and conditions of employment and the rights and responsibilities of both parties, and specified that a minimum wage would be honored unless the prevailing wage was higher.

Watson B. Miller, Commissioner of Immigration and Naturalization, was a delegate at the El Paso meetings in November 1947 and interpreted the new agreement to mean unlimited importation of Mexican contract labor without the restraint of a quota. The quota, which had been set by Mexico at 100,000 by the end of the war, was never reached, for the United States consistently failed to recruit the allotted number of workers. Miller on April 6, 1948, authorized the importation of Mexican agricultural workers for temporary employment. On July 3, 1948, Congress enacted Public Law 893 authorizing the Federal Security Agency to recruit foreign workers and direct the program through June 30, 1949. Public Law 893 appropriated $2,500,000 for the program, which, being miniscule in comparison to earlier appropriations, demonstrated the basic "hands off" policy of the United States in financing, supervising and guiding the labor operation.[14] The Farm Placement Service of the USES, which was involved in farm labor matters, was transferred from the Department of Labor to the Federal Security Agency. Under the 1949 agreement, when the government did inject itself into the alien labor situation, it was generally through the Farm Placement Service of the USES, the Immigration and Naturalization Service, the Department of Labor and the Department of State.[15]

From February to early fall in 1948, the binational labor program functioned quietly and efficiently with some 30,000 contract workers imported under the aegis of the 1948 Mexican-United States agreement.[16] The agreement came unglued as the interrelated problems of wetbacks, placement of contracting centers and the ban of workers to Texas undermined United States agribusiness and government support of the program.

Mexico continued to oppose border recruitment, with centers being established at Tampico and Aguascalientes, cities respectively 500 and 655 miles from Laredo, Texas, or about 1200 and 900 miles south of El Paso, Texas. After continued United States pressure, Mexico agreed to establish a single border recruitment center at Mexicali, Mexico, just across the international border from Calexico, California. This Mexican compromise precipitated unabated United States demands for blanket border recruitment from California to the Gulf of Mexico.[17]

The Secret Study revealed that negotiations were held in Mexico City from August 2 to August 3, 1948, resulting in further Mexican concessions. The recruiting locations were moved northward to Chihuahua, a distance of only 235 miles from El Paso; Monterrey, 145 miles from Laredo; and Culiacan, 600 miles to the south of Nogales, Arizona. The Mexicali center continued to operate.[18] The Chihuahua center was never established because the governor of the State of Chihuahua demurred by asserting local manpower needs were too pressing to allow the emigration of its workers. Consequently, the USES informed the State Department that farmers would use wetbacks and advocated unilateral United States disruption of the 1948 pact.

> The government should immediately give serious consideration
> to admitting to the United States, Mexican agricultural labor-
> ers ... without regard to the agreement. ... The agreement
> should be denounced ... in as much as the agreement has been
> found unworkable.[19]

The USES, which was the key agency in determining domestic need for foreign labor, opted for an open border in direct violation of the Mexican-United States Agreement, the United States immigration laws and Mexican statute law, which prohibited unbridled illegal emigration of its farm workers. Organized labor violently objected to the position typified by USES and agribusiness interests.

Henry L. Mitchell, president of the National Farm Labor Union, asserted that thousands of illegal workers were entering Texas, Arizona and California, and undercutting domestic worker wage rates. Mitchell claimed Mexican labor was beneficial only in building the cheap labor empire of the gigantic agribusiness industry. Mitchell, in testimony before a Senate Judiciary Sub-committee conducting hearings from non-governmental groups on immigration, averred that the entire alien farm worker program should be scrapped for it was subverting the principle of providing work for willing and able Americans.[20]

Henry A. Wallace, Progressive Party Candidate for the presidency in 1948, described agribusiness leaders on a campaign tour in California as "absentee landlords, land speculators and oil kings". In making these accusations Wallace was supporting the NFLU strike against Joseph DiGiorgio which commenced on October 1, 1947. DiGorgio owned the largest farm in California's Central Valley and had received $1,000,000 from the Bank of America to fight union attempts to improve working conditions and organize farm workers.[21]

Despite the fact that the United States was a party to an international agreement of which Section 29 provided for international containment of wetback labor, there emerged an interagency meeting to discuss the pros and cons of a permanent opening of the Mexican-United States border.[22] The Labor Department supported such activity and the Immigration and Naturalization Service concurred, provided that the influx was manageable and easily apportioned among the farmers and growers. The Department of State objected to opening the border because it violated an international agreement and could lead to adverse diplomatic repercussions. As frequently happens when government agencies severely disagree on policy, the White House arbitrated the disputes. At a meeting at the White House on September 22, 1948, Presidential Administrative Assistant David Stowe indicated that the President would not support a violation of the agreement or its termination.[23]

However, on the weekend of October 16-17, 1948, the Texas-Mexican border at El Paso, Texas and Ciudad Juarez, Mexico, was opened to any Mexican desiring admittance. The Associated Press reported that the United States immigration and Naturalization Service opened the border to an estimated 4,000 Mexicans and distributed them to farmers in New Mexico and Texas, thereby abandoning attempts to prevent the illegal entrance of desperately impoverished Mexican farm workers.[24]

The Mexican reaction was swift. That nation declared on October 18, 1948, that the El Paso incident indicated the United States had unilaterally abrogated the international agreement of February 21, 1948, and presented a four-point protest to the State Department. The points were as follows: first, it expressed the profound disappointment of the Mexican Government with the untoward position assumed by United States immigration authorities; second, it informed the United States that because of this position, Mexico was ending the agreement of February 17, 1948; third, it refused, from that time on, all responsibility for termination of the pact; fourth, it indicated that the Mexican Government reserved the right to claim retribution for damages the United States Immigration Service's determination might cause to the economy of the nation and to its nationals. Mexico, in addition, recalled Alfonso Guerra, who had been on a fact-finding tour of southwestern and western work camps.[25]

Two days after the abrogation, I and NS denied that the border was opened to Mexicans. Deputy Immigration Commissioner John B. Boyd asserted that the Immigration Service never gave blanket authority allowing the indiscriminate entrance of wetbacks.[26] The crisis resulted in a special meeting at the White House on October 22, 1948, in which the White House Staff member expressed "surprise" that the USES and I and NS had willfully and knowingly violated the agreement.[27] A note was promptly drafted and presented to the Mexican Embassy that afternoon which officially regretted the incident. The note specifically expressed "profound regret" for violating Section 29 of the agreement, declared the border would now be tightly inspected, and the illegals repatriated to Mexico. In addition, the United States guaranteed to protect the rights of those legally contracted workers.[28] The following day, October 23, 1948, Mexico accepted as satisfactory the United States apology for precipitating the El Paso crisis.[29]

There is no question that the United States disregarded the international boundary provisions of the agreement and acted in an imperial and outlandish manner. Grover C. Wilmoth, District Director of the I and NS, who was an adviser to the United States negotiating team at the El Paso Conference in November-December 1947, opened the border for illegal migrants because "they need the work, our farmers need them and the crops were going to waste". Robert Goodwin claimed at hearings before the Bureau of the Budget that the "El Paso incident was created by him on the allegation that the present treaty is not working in that we were not getting needed farm labor from Mexico."[31] It seems certain no direct order emanated from the White House to open the border, for the president was critical of USES and I and NS laxity in honoring international agreements. The United States Embassy in Mexico interpreted, however, the El Paso incident as a result of governmental indifference to arbitrary employer decision-making. The Embassy desired a return to the wartime program in which the Executive Branch was more actively involved in the implementation of the program.[32]

There was no excuse for United States abandonment of an international agreement for however brief a period. This breach was a dramatic and highly visible form of United States subversion of international law, but it must be emphasized that four to seven thousand illegals was a small addition to an already burgeoning Mexican wetback population. There were approximately 100,000 Mexican nationals illegally in Texas alone by October, 1948, and this figure represented twice the number of legally contracted braceros.[33] A border inspector patrolman maintained that the illegal influx into Texas was approaching 115-120 a day before the El Paso incident.[34] The crisis at El Paso was insignificant in terms of the number of admitted wetbacks but important as an example of an arrogant display of disrespect for an agreement with a foreign power.

Although Mexican acceptance of the United States' apology came too rapidly for agreement actually to be abrogated, efforts began to materialize to hammer out still another agreement. In November, 1948, twenty states sent agricultural employers to meetings in Saint Louis, San Francisco and Denver to discuss both the 1948 binational agreement and individual work contract and to discuss desirable changes that would appear in any new agreement. In December the Special Farm Labor Committee met in Washington, D.C. This agricultural advisory group, consisting of an agricultural representative from each state, offered and adopted a resolution creating a Special Committee on Mexican Labor to pursue the problem of developing a new Agreement and Contract. This committee met in December 1948 with the USES, I and NS, and Department of State, and drew up a draft of a new work contract which in turn was submitted to the Inter-departmental Committee on Foreign Labor and back again to the Special Committee on Mexican Labor.[35]

During this interim period between the El Paso affair and the drawing up of a new agreement, the United States advocated the legalization of wetbacks. This drying out of wetbacks had initially taken place under the two supplementary agreements of March 10, 1947. The agreement which directly legalized wetbacks in Texas had been abrogated by Mexico on March 10, 1947, and the other agreement of 1947 which dealt with wetbacks in general had been superseded by the 1948 pact, which eliminated the legalization process.[36] The latter agreement prevented wetbacks from being legalized for employment because both governments had then concluded that the result would be a mammoth uncontrollable wetback migration. Now both nations toyed with the idea of establishing a cutoff date in which all wetbacks in the United States could be eligible for legal employment. They agreed that

January 7, 1949, would be the cutoff date; they also reaffirmed other provisions of the 1948 agreement until its replacement.[37]

Full scale negotiations were conducted in Mexico City from January 15 to February 17, 1949, in which arrangements governing contracting of Mexican farm workers were discussed. The United States explained the failure of the 1948 agreement as the result of the Texas ban and Mexican adherence to interior recruiting. The United States insisted that eradication of the wetback traffic was contingent upon removal of the Texas ban and the establishment of joint determination of blacklisted areas. Mexico cited the wetback as the principal disruptive factor and surprisingly advocated that a new 1949 agreement "should include a provision for the regularization of workers now illegally in the United States ... this should be the principal basis of the agreement."[38] Mexico wanted the interim legalization agreement of January 7, 1949, to become the capstone of the new long-term agreement.

Prior to the current round of negotiations, the United States delegation had agreed that should Mexico reiterate its interior recruitment position, the United States would suggest the establishment of recruitment centers on a line between Hermosillo through Torreon to Monterrey--a maximum distance of 600 miles from the international border. When Mexico actually offered this plan, USES officials uncompromisingly threatened to recess the talks.[39] Mexico stuck to its position and the United States delegation departed from Mexico on February 17, 1949, without establishing border recruitment or arranging a binational agreement after thirty days of negotiations.[40]

Another major cause for the breakdown of negotiations was Mexico's insistence upon unilateral blacklisting and determination of places of employment. Mexico demanded that a blacklisted area would remain so until the following conditions could be met: first, the principal county and municipal authorities of the towns nearest the area involved had to furnish a written guarantee, in the name of the community, that Mexicans would not suffer any discrimination; second, state and federal authorities also had to guarantee that there would be no discrimination; third, if discrimination did nevertheless occur, the Mexican Consul in the area was to request the USES to initiate a joint investigation. Should discrimination be verified, the employer-worker contracts were cancelled. If the USES and the Mexican Consul differed as to the presence of discrimination, the issue should be unilaterally resolved by the Mexican Foreign Minister. In early summer, 1949, the State Department informed Mexico that there would not be any binational agreement if Mexico continued to insist upon unilateral blacklisting.[41] This time Mexico caved in to United States demands and accepted the principle of joint determination, resulting in lifting of the Texas ban.

Only border recruitment remained as an obstacle for a new bilateral agreement. This issue had caused the negotiations to break off and was only resolved with United States acquiescence. The State Department, which was critical of Mexican demands for unilateral blacklisting, supported the Mexican position on border recruitment. The State Department feared unlimited border contracting might accelerate the wetback influx; the Department also contended that interior recruiting was not beyond the financial means of the employer.[42] Even the arch-conservative Special Committee on Mexican Labor, whose employer members had close ties with USES and I and NS officials, was willing to give up its demand for border recruiting for the committee and "indicated the agreement should not fall on that score."[43] The United States, in accepting the principal of interior recruiting, cleared the way for both nations to sign yet another agreement on July 29, 1949, which became formalized three days later through an exchange of notes.[44]

A major provision of the agreement was the legalization of all wetbacks who were in the United States on or before August 1, 1949, the effective date of the agreement. These men were preferentially hired over other Mexicans seeking their first admission into the United States. Both nations pledged to inhibit subsequent wetback traffic and declared that any illegal entry after August 1 would not be legalized but promptly repatriated to Mexico.[45] This policy led to granting contract status to 87,220 wetbacks who were in the United States before the cutoff date. This certification of wetbacks renewed in part the policy of the March, 1947, agreements which had been temporarily suspended by the bilateral agreement of 1948.

With regard to discrimination, the 1948 agreement merely provided that Mexican workers should not be the object of prejudice; the 1949 agreement, in combining proposals put forth by the Mexican Government and the Texas Employment Commission, placed the responsibility for safeguarding the workers' rights upon the respective communities.[46] The agreement provided for the denial of Mexican labor to areas where discrimination existed.

The agreement provided for joint determination which eliminated previous unilateral blacklisting practices. Before workers could enter the United States for a particular locale, Mexico would notify the USES through the United States Embassy, if the area in question was suspected of discriminating against Mexicans. Instead of an outright Mexican ban of the area, the USES investigated the allegation and, if it corroborated the Mexican suspicion, the United States Immigration and Naturalization Service would prevent the entrance of Mexicans.[47] If the USES disagreed with Mexican accusations of discrimination, the Mexican Consulate of the particular area in question could require officials of the community to sign a pledge that no discriminatory acts would occur. If rumors of maltreatment persisted after the community pledges, the local officials would have to investigate and remedy any situation which violated the pledge. The Mexican Government agreed to allow employment of its nationals in locations where pledges were obtained.

If Mexican nationals employed on the basis of such pledges became objects of community prejudice, the Mexican Consulate could request a joint United States-Mexican investigation. Should the bilateral investigation determine that the community non-discrimination pledges had been violated, the Individual Work Contracts were terminated, with the subsequent removal of all the afflicted Mexican nationals. Should the USES and Mexican Consul differ as to the presence of discrimination, the 1949 agreement vaguely provided for the disposal of such problems through diplomatic channels.[48]

The immediate effect of joint determination of discrimination was the revocation of the Texas ban. Except from March to October, 1947, Mexico had prohibited its citizens from performing agricultural tasks in that state.[49]

The 1948 agreement had specified that Mexico reserve the right to establish recruitment centers at places of its own choosing provided they were not south of Guadalajara and Queretaro. This was a major source of disagreement during the period of the 1948 pact. Mexico succeeded again in preventing border recruitment of its nationals, but, unlike previous agreements, the actual locations were written into the agreement. The places of contracting were Hermosillo, Sonora; Chihuahua, Chihuahua; and Monterrey, Nuevo Leon. USES had the authority to determine which United States employers could contract at these contract centers provided that the employer was permitted to contract labor at the nearest center.[50]

The 1949 Farm Labor Agreement contained compliance procedures. This was the first agreement which required drafting a Joint Interpretation to clarify in greater detail the Mexican-United States official interpretation. A system of periodic inspections was established with USES and I and NS representatives responsible for on-the-job inspections; a system of violations investigations was also established.[51]

Joint determination was the guiding principle for determining compliance. This was manifested in the agreement in which "no unilateral interpretation made either by the United States Employment Service representative or the Mexican Consulate shall be binding upon the parties to the Individual Work Contract unless jointly ratified by the two governments." There was joint determination for any problem if the Mexican Consulate requested; if not, USES would resolve the complaint alone, notifying the Consulate of the decision. If a joint determination failed at consensus, the case was referred to the appropriate Mexican Consul General and the Bureau of Employment Security Regional Representative.[52] Should the latter bodies fail to agree on the proper disposition, however, the agreement provided no further mechanism for resolution. According to the Secret Study, the agreement required that "in all cases the status quo was to be maintained."[53] This statement appears in Section 22, "The employer and the worker shall continue to be bound by the provisions of the contract while the conciliation procedure is in process."

The 1949 migratory worker pact dropped the 10% savings fund deduction which had appeared in previous agreements. Except for the above, major provisions of the 1948 agreement were preserved. The employer had to finance lodgings and transportation; had to guarantee employment 75% of the contract period and had to pay the prevailing wage. The agreement sustained the important principle of direct employer-to-worker contracts despite persistent Mexican demands for a revival of the wartime government-to-government contracts in which the United States was directly responsible for contract compliance. Neither the 1948 or 1949 binational agreements had a termination date, although either nation could abrogate each upon thirty days notice.

The Secret Study contained a United States Embassy summary of the problems which arose under the 1949 Agreement. There were essentially five critical problem areas. First, the Embassy report indicated that Texas employers had committed mass violations with regard to recruiting, wages, general living conditions and utilization of non-contract labor. Second, the USES was not enforcing certain wage requirements and assumed a partial attitude in favor of agribusiness interests. Third, Mexicans were illegally denied their three-fourths work guarantees when employers hired domestic labor. Article 9 of the Individual Work Contract provided that if the "employer affords the worker ... less employment ... the worker shall be paid the amount which he would have earned had he, in fact, worked for the guaranteed number of days."[54] Contracts terminated through no fault of the worker did not permit the denial of wages. Fourth, employers were returning workers to Mexico without previously informing the Mexican Consuls, despite Consular protestations that such activity made it difficult to determine if there had been any outstanding complaints against the employer. Fifth, the Embassy report concluded with the episode of unjustified imprisonment of Mexicans in an incident in Tivoli, Texas.[55]

Compliance remained the central problem. Employers were generally dissatisfied with the 1949 International Agreement and Work Contract. Less than a month after the agreements and contracts were consummated, agribusiness interests began to lobby intensively for a renegotiation. Keith Mets, Chairman of the powerful Growers Committee from California, Arizona, New Mexico and Texas, urged the President to establish border recruitment. Mets, also a member of the Special Committee on Mexican Labor, knew quite well that Mexico would destroy any agreement if the United States unilaterally introduced border hiring practices. The Growers Committee also requested the contracting of illegal workers whenever apprehended and the arbitrary firing of workers without a full hearing.[56] Truman replied with the reminder that Mexico would not open contracting centers at border points and stated the official government position that any legalization of wetbacks after August 1, 1949, "would be a permanent invitation for Mexican Nationals to cross the border illegally in order to obtain employment in this country."[57] Truman also attacked Mets' proposal of unilateral firing of workers on the grounds that the pact prevented unilateral termination of contract by the Mexican Government or employer.[58]

In spite of a presidential rebuke, Mets and other big-farm people had a powerful constituency in the Congress which kept up the pressure to ignore or renegotiate the 1949 Mexican farm labor agreement. Sheridan Downey, Senator from California, echoed the demands of the agribusiness industry in the Imperial Valley for border recruitment, permanent legalization of wetbacks, and arbitrary dismissal of Mexican national employees. Downey, in supporting Mets' organization, specifically mentioned Mets in his letter to Truman indicating the powerful influence of farm grower interests.[59]

Clinton P. Anderson, Senator from New Mexico, relayed a telegram to the president from one of "the biggest farmers" in New Mexico. Anderson endorsed the farmers' position that wetbacks should not be deported regardless of their arrival date into the United States and described the Individual Work Contract as "unworkable."[60]

Anderson had previously introduced into Congress a bill which would have created indiscriminate Mexican migration into the United States. Anderson's bill S 272, attempted "to facilitate the admission of certain foreign workers desiring to perform agricultural work in the United States."[61] This bill, while never passed, was significant in polarizing opinion from those in favor of an open border to those advocating the honoring of an international agreement which directly outlawed illegal immigration. The Department of State, which consistently fought congressional or federal agency attempts to subvert the labor pact, protested against the Anderson Bill's provision that the only prerequisite to importing Mexican labor would

be the Department of Agriculture's certification of a labor need. In a tersely worded letter to the Senate Judiciary Subcommittee, which was conducting
hearings on the legislation, Assistant Secretary of State Ernest Gross predicted
that, if passed, "it is highly probable that our relations with Mexico would be
adversely affected."[62] The Federal Security Agency also deplored the measure
because it callously failed to establish housing, health and minimum wage standards for the braceros.[63]

The USES, which consistently sided with vested agricultural interests,
objected only to the provision dealing with the Agriculture Department, for the
former agency had been the sole certifier of labor needs and wanted to retain this
function. Director Robert Goodwin informed Secretary of Labor Maurice J. Tobin
that employers in general and the Special Farm Labor Committee in particular were
"unanimous" in their preference for the Anderson bill, which would permit the
employment of "any Mexican in this country."[64]

There were other attempts at introducing open border legislation. The
Federal Security Administrator drafted a bill to guarantee permanent legislation
for importing alien labor. The Department of Labor severely criticized the FSA
draft on the grounds that unemployment in the summer of 1949 was on the increase,
and referred to a Bureau of Agricultural Economics' report that increasing agricultural mechanization was displacing human labor.[65] Secretary of Labor Tobin,
in a letter to Budget Bureau Director Frank Pace, predicted that permanent legislation would "give rise to strong and continuing pressures by interested groups
...in securing an influx of foreign labor in excess of actual needs even when
domestic labor may be sufficiently available."[66]

While both bills reflected a desire to ease immigration restrictions,
there were interest groups fighting to tighten them.

The American Federation of Labor, through its member National Farm
Labor Union, requested a total cessation of alien labor because it was running
domestic labor off the land and creating thousands of poverty-ridden citizens.
The union successfully enlisted the support of the Federal Advisory Council of
the Bureau of Employment Security, Department of Labor. The Federal Advisory
Council contained labor, employer, veteran and public representatives. The
Council advocated an end to the bracero program.

> We recommend that no international agreements be negoti-
> ated or any other arrangements be made during the coming
> year for recruitment of foreign workers and ... the USES
> withdraw all certifications of need for foreign agricul-
> tural workers.[67]

Shortly after the Council's decision, organized labor intensified its
criticism of the 1949 agreement. Ernesto Galarza, one of the most articulate anti-
agribusiness labor spokesmen, charged that the foreign labor program was cutting
domestic wages from ninety cents to fifty cents an hour in central California.
He reasoned that the attempts to legalize only those wetbacks who were in the
United States on August 1, 1949, was impossible due to the unannounced nature of
the wetback's arrival to the United States. Galarza, who served as Director of

Research and Education of the NFLU, urged that labor representatives help determine the certification of need for foreign labor. The USES could be stripped of its sole discretionary power in this area with the introduction of public hearings and thorough investigations of domestic labor availability.[68]

The NFLU adopted a resolution at its sixteenth annual convention in Fresno, California, urging Congress to enact legislation that would penalize any employer hiring wetbacks. Due to the bankruptcy of the cutoff date as a deterrent to further wetback migration, employers, according to the union, had to be intimidated from hiring this labor.[69]

The forces advocating an end to the bracero program used the United Nations as a forum for discussion. Rowland Watts, National Secretary of the Workers Defense League, appeared before a special United Nations committee on slavery and delivered a list of charges on behalf of the Commission of Inquiry into Forced Labor entitled, "Legal and Illegal Forms of Forced Labor in the United States". He told the Committee that illegal immigrants were exploited by farmers and accused the United States of failing to supervise adequately the wage scales and working conditions of Mexican contract labor during the Second World War. The system of using Mexican labor continued in the postwar world, according to Watts, in spite of a sufficient supply of domestic farm labor. Watts claimed that 200,000 wetbacks entered the United States annually and that between August and September, 1949, 118,575 Mexican nationals were imported and distributed to 570 large farms.[70]

While open border and closed border advocates were debating their positions, strikes began to occur throughout California. The strike was a major NFLU weapon in their organizational campaign to recruit more members and to force the agribusiness industry into improving wage and work conditions for the workers. Strikes in the Imperial Valley, the Central Valley and the San Joaquin Valley had plunged the West Coast farm situation into turbulence by the spring of 1950.[71]

The DiGiorgio ranch strike, which was in its fourth year, was the object of a House Labor Committee on-the-spot investigation of union charges concerning horrendous living conditions. Two of its more prominent members were Representatives Richard M. Nixon of California and Thurston B. Morton of Kentucky. Along with other committee members, they concluded that the NFLU misrepresented DiGiorgio's conditions of employment in "a shocking collection of falsehoods almost wholly unrelieved by any regard whatever for the truth and the facts."[72]

Edward S. Benet, United States Consul in Reynosa, a Mexican border town, described the Texas farm labor situation as a threat to diplomatic relations with Mexico.[73] Benet felt the cheap labor needs of farmers were less important than the maintenance of strong relations with Mexico. Cheap labor was creating an unequal distribution of wealth; a few had enriched themselves through the use of this cheap labor but the majority were working for depressed wages in a semi-feudal order. Texas farmers, for example, refused to pay a minimum wage of forty cents an hour despite Mexican claims that the then-present wage of twenty-five cents an hour was inadequate. Benet, reflecting the State Department position, opposed an open border on the grounds of possible injury to Mexican-United States relations and its denial of Mexican labor to non-border states. With an unusual use of metaphor for a State Department officer, Benet wrote Walter Thurston, Ambassador to Mexico, that "the kettle is really boiling and the tempest gives promise to increase in its intensity."[74]

Amid strikes, congressional accusations of union distortions, and charges and countercharges between open and closed border advocates, the Mexican Government informed the United States in June, 1950, that any new recruitment would have to come solely from Mexicans illegally in the United States. In an exchange of notes on July 26, 1950, a new cutoff date for legalizing wetbacks was created on July 27, 1950.[75] Obviously reflecting the failure to prevent illegal migratory labor from entering the United States, wetbacks who had ignored the previous cutoff date of August 1, 1949, were now eligible under the third cutoff date of July 27, 1950.

The August, 1949, bracero pact contained the following declaration: both nations would "take all necessary measures to suppress radically the illegal traffic of Mexican workers." In 1947 and 1949, Mexico hoped that wetback legalization under a cutoff date would deter future wetbacks and provide intergovernmental protection for newly legalized contract workers. With 10,000 Mexicans entering California illegally each month and 20,000 entering along the border between Texas and New Mexico, Mexico suggested that no more workers be directly recruited from Mexico.[76] A weak gesture, indeed, when one considers that any Mexican could enter the United States and eventually be legalized.

Another indication of the program's deterioration emerged when Mexico reversed its seven-year position against border contracting centers by permitting on August 18, 1950, the issuance of work certificates to Mexican workers at the border.[77] Two months later Mexico insisted all future recruiting would come again from wetbacks in the United States. This time, the July 27, 1950, cutoff date was not replaced. The triumph of the open border had been secured. Mexico staunch protagonist of an unprotected international border, consented to recruitment among wetbacks regardless of their date of entry. Although Mexico expressed concern about the total withdrawal of wetback restraint, there was no abrogation; there was no protest note--just a request that publicity of the Mexican-supported open border "be restricted".[78]

1947-50 NADIR

Mexico had lost its battle to contain the flow of its labor to the United States. The growers and their congressional allies achieved their objective of eliminating any regulations or restraint upon hiring Mexican braceros. The USES and I and NS sympathized with those interests since the USES was derelict in its duty of certifying the need for alien labor and the I and NS demonstrated at El Paso its utter disregard for the Mexican-United States agreement.

The unions were handicapped from the start. They had no governmental public interested or powerful enough to secure the border. The State Department, which should be credited for its refusal to support agri-business interests, did not succeed in closing the border, because it was not the department's responsibility. The White House supported the binational agreements but was passive in their enforcement. There were no reprisals against officials who created the El Paso incident; there was no executive pressure for tough legislation to penalize the harboring, concealing or hiring of wetbacks. The demise of the binational bracero program resulted in a near unanimous cry for a President's Commission on Migratory Labor to exhaustively investigate and recommend solutions to restore order to a totally bankrupt Mexican-United States labor importation program.

Footnotes:

1. "The Executive Agreement, 1948", Secret Study, Stowe Papers, Truman Library. The David H. Stowe papers in the Truman Library contain a four-chapter secret study of the inter-American labor program. Much of these chapters were drawn from State Department Files 811.504 and 811.06M, from 1948 to 1953. Certain references were omitted and the officials involved remained anonymous. This study was untitled but the chapters were not. No author or date of publication was given, but I have deduced that it was written between March 23, 1954 and December 31, 1955. Hereafter, the citations will include abbreviated chapter title, Secret Study, and page.

2. 62 Stat. 3887.

3. Ibid., pp. 3887-3888. The United States delegates were William G. Maclean. Economic Adviser, Division of Mexican Affairs, Department of State; Watson B. Miller, Commissioner of Immigration and Naturalization, Department of Justice; Willard Kelly, Assistant Commissioner of Immigration and Naturalization; Walter Erb, Acting Assistant Director for Farm Placement, United States Employment Service, Department of Labor. Mexican Delegates were Alfonso Guerra, Executive Officer of the Department of Foreign Affairs; Horacio Teran, Executive Officer of the Department of the Interior; Colonel Raul Michel, Consul General of Mexico at El Paso, Texas; Elso Ledesma Labastida, Chief Counselor, Department of Labor and Social Welfare.

4. "Agreement, 1948", Secret Study, pp. 3-5

5. 62 Stat. 3889.

6. New York Times, December 8, 1947 (hereafter referred to as NYT).

7. NYT, January 22, 1948. The NCA is a non-profit organization representing 750 canners and producing seventy-five per cent of the annual volume of these commodities.

8. Ibid.

9. 62 Stat. 3888.

10. The agreement may be found in 62 Stat. 3887-3894.

11. Memorandum, T. J. Kalis to R. L. Goodwin, April 13, 1948, cited in "Agreement, 1948", Secret Study, p. 6.

12. Daniel Gott, "Employment of Foreign Workers in United States Agriculture", The Department of State Bulletin, July 18, 1949, p. 45.

13. NYT, December 8, 1947.

14. 62 Stat. 1238-39, 80th Congress, 2d Session, July 3, 1948. Public Law 893 was passed by Congress on June 21, 1938. NYT, June 21, 1948.

15. *Chronology of Recruitment of Mexican Workers for Agricultural Employment in the United States, 1941-1951*, Chronological File: January 1, 1951-June 4, 1951 Folder, Records of the President's Commission on Migratory Labor, Truman Library.

16. "Information Relative to Temporary Admission of Nationals of Mexico to the United States to Engage in Agricultural Employment under the Agreement of August 1, 1949 Governing the Migration of Mexican Agricultural Workers." Issued Jointly by Commissioner of Immigration and Naturalization and Director of United States Employment Service, August 1949.

17. "Agreement, 1948", *Secret Study*, p. 10.

18. *Ibid.*

19. *Ibid.*, pp. 11-12.

20. *NYT*, August 1, 1948.

21. *NYT*, October 4, 1948.

22. 62 *Stat.* 3892.

23. "Agreement, 1948", *Secret Study*, p. 12; Memorandum, David K. Niles to the President, June 8, 1949, Nash Files, Truman Papers, Truman Library. The memorandum reveals that the White House officials involved with the labor program were Stowe and Dr. John Steelman. The agreement provided abrogation on thirty days notice.

24. *NYT*, October 17, 1948. The *Secret Study* estimated that between 5,000-7,000 entered from Ciudad Juarez, Mexico.

25. *The Department of State Bulletin*, November 7, 1948, 585-86; *NYT*, October 19, 1948.

26. *NYT*, October 21, 1948.

27. "Agreement, 1948", *Secret Study*, p. 15.

28. *Documents on American Foreign Relations*, 1948, p. 537.

29. *Ibid.*, p. 538

30. *NYT*, October 19, 1948.

31. Byron Mitchell, *Memorandum Report: Immigration from Mexico*, December 31, 1948, Migratory Labor Folder, Department of Labor, Office of Secretary, Assistant Secretary John W. Gibson (RG 174), National Archives.

32. "Agreement, 1948", *Secret Study*, p. 15.

33. Mitchell, *Immigration*, p. 1.

34. NYT, September 7, 1948.

35. Robert C. Goodwin to the Secretary of Labor, August 26, 1949, 1949 Bureau of Employment Security Folder, Department of Labor, Office of the Secretary, Secretary Maurice J. Tobin (RB 174), National Archives.

36. Chronology, p. 7; Otey M. Scruggs, "Texas and the Bracero Program", Pacific Northwest Review, February 1963, p. 263.

37. "The International Agreement: 1949-1950", Secret Study, p. 2.

38. Ibid., p. 3.

39. Ibid., p. 4.

40. Goodwin to Secretary of Labor, August 26, 1949; The Department of State Bulletin, January 23, 1949, p. 116. United States delegates were: Leslie A. Wheeler, Counselor of United States Embassy, Mexico City; Cleon Swayzee, Chief, Division of International Labor and Social Affairs, Department of State; Robert E. Wilson, Acting Assistant Chief, Division of Mexican Affairs, Department of State; Watson B. Miller, Commissioner of Immigration and Naturalization; Louis Blanchard, American Vice Consul, Mexico City; Don Larin, Chief of Farm Placement, Bureau of Employment Security, Federal Security Agency; Albert Misler, Office of the General Counsel, Federal Security Agency; Oscar Harper, Farm Placement Representative in San Francisco, Bureau of Employment Security, Federal Security Agency, The Special Committee on Mexican Labor, a subcommittee of the Special Farm Labor Advisory Committee, served as an advisor to the United States delegation.

41. "Agreement: 1949-50", Secret Study, pp. 5-6.

42. Ibid., p. 6.

43. Goodwin to Secretary of labor, August 26, 1949.

44. The signatories were Leslie A. Wheeler for the American delegation and Alfonso Guerra for the Mexican.

45. United States Department of State, TIAS 2260, United States Treaties and Other International Acts, Series 2260, pp. 2-20; hereafter cited as TIAS.

46. Ibid.

47. George O. Coalson, "Mexican Contract Labor in American Agriculture", Southwestern Social Science Quarterly (December 1952), pp. 228-238.

48. Joint Interpretations of the International Executive Agreement by Governments of Mexico and the United States, pp. 42-61, TIAS, 2260.

49. NYT, July 30, 1949; NYT, August 28, 1949.

50. International Executive Agreement (Mexico-United States Farm Labor Agreement), OF 407-D, Truman Papers, Truman Library.

51. Joint Interpretation of the International Executive Agreement by the Governments of Mexico and the United States, OF 407-D, Truman Papers, Truman Library.

52. Ibid.

53. "Agreement: 1949-50", Secret Study, p. 9a.

54. The Individual Work Contract, TIAS 2260.

55. Agreement: 1949-50", Secret Study, pp. 10-11.

56. Keith Mets to the President, August 18, 1949, OF 407-D, Truman Papers, Truman Library; 57 Harry S. Truman to Mets, August 22, 1949, of 407-D, Truman Papers, Truman Library. In my copy, the President spelled the recipient's last name with a "z" which was incorrect. Mets signed his name with an "s".

57. Ibid.

58. Ibid.

59. Sheridan Downey to John R. Steelman, August 25, 1949, OF 407-D, Truman Papers, Truman Library.

60. Clinton P. Anderson to the President, August 24, 1949, OF 407-D. Truman Papers, Truman Library.

61. Congressional Record, 95: 84.

62. NYT, July 13, 1949. If passed, Truman might not have vetoed it despite his general aversion to the grower lobby. In a "Dear Clint" letter, Truman wrote Anderson, his former Secretary of Agriculture (1945-1948), that the 1949 Individual Worker Contract "certainly was written by someone without much sense of practical approach." This was the only letter in his papers which criticized the 1949 agreement or contract. See: Truman to Anderson, August 26, 1949, of 407-D, Truman Papers, Truman Library.

63. NYT, July 13, 1949.

64. Goodwin to Secretary of Labor, August 25, 1949.

65. Secretary of Labor to Frank Pace, June 6, 1949, Budget Bureau Folder, Department of Labor, Office of the Secretary, Secretary Tobin (RG 174), National Archives.

66. Ibid.

67. NYT, December 17, 1949.

68. Ernesto Galarza, "Mexican-United States Labor Relations and Problems", January 25, 1950, Los Angeles, California, August 10-12, 1950, Statements #1 Folder, Records of the President's Commission on Migratory Labor, Truman Library.

69. NYT, January 15, 1950; NYT, February 26, 1950.

70. NYT, March 3, 1950.

71. NYT, May 21, 1950.

72. NYT, March 11, 1950.

73. Edward S. Benet to Walter Thurston, October 5, 1949, OF 407-D, Truman Papers, Truman Library.

74. Ibid.

75. "Agreement: 1949-50", Secret Study, pp. 12-13; Coalson, "Mexican Contract Labor", p. 234.

76. NYT, March 28, 1950. Figures cited from an article by Gladwin Hill, a Times reporter who wrote extensively on the Mexican farm labor program.

77. "Agreement: 1949-50", Secret Study, pp. 13-14.

78. Ibid.

CHAPTER VI

PRESIDENT'S COMMISSION ON MIGRATORY LABOR

As the intergovernmental migrant labor program became increasingly un-
popular and unworkable, farm, labor and civil rights groups clamored for a Presidential Commission to investigate and study the entire spectrum of domestic and
alien migrant labor. With the addition of some government agencies advocating
the establishment of such a commission, the administration began to seriously
consider the possibility in the winter of 1949.

Roy Wilkins, Acting Secretary of the National Association for the Advancement of Colored People, advanced the commission concept in order to focus public attention upon the miserable conditions of those who planted and harvested
agricultural commodities. Wilkins attacked the foreign labor importation program
as a means to undermine domestic farm worker strikes for better wages and governmental protection of their rights.[1]

Assistant Secretary of Labor John W. Gibson desired the establishment
of a Presidential Commission and used reports of police brutality against Mexicans as a lobbying device to achieve it. The Budget Bureau received agency recommendations for a Commission and was responsible for advising the President as to
the merits of such a proposal.[2] On November 5, 1949, in a letter to Norman Thomas,
President Harry S. Truman revealed that the Department of Labor was considering the
feasibility of a Presidential Commission on Agricultural Problems.[3] Truman informed Thomas, a prominent Socialist and perennial presidential candidate, that
whether or not such a commission were established, his administration had pledged
itself to utilize domestic labor before hiring foreign labor; to explore the problems of adequate living conditions of migrant labor; and to generally uplift migratory labor conditions.[4]

The President indicated that if a Presidential Commission on Agricultural
Problems were established, it would study closely the conditions of "colored
people" involved in the problems of migrancy.[5] If a commission were not created,
the Executive branch would be "continuously interested in fostering policies which
will improve the working conditions and opportunities of our colored citizens
who are engaged in agricultural activity."[6]

Helen Gahagan Douglas, Democratic Congresswoman from California, claimed
that Mexican labor was creating economic chaos in California's Imperial Valley by
exacerbating the domestic unemployment situation. Truman, in what was becoming a
ritualistic response to critics of the bracero program, informed Douglas that a commission was under close study and, in any event, that his administration would
protect the interests of domestic migrants by limiting foreign labor importation
whether a commission would recommend it or not.[7]

By the spring of 1950, a proposed executive order to establish a commission had been drafted by Peyton Ford, Acting Attorney General, and revised by Frederick J. Lawton, Budget Bureau Director.[8] The proposed draft was also discussed with representatives of the Department of Labor, State, Agriculture, the Immigration and Naturalization Service and the Federal Security Agency.[9]

There was not unanimous approval of the proposed executive order. Attorney General J. Howard McGrath wanted to defer the appointment of a migratory labor commission because the executive order was too comprehensive in encompassing both alien and domestic migratory labor. McGrath suggested that if such a commission were established, it should be allowed to submit its final report beyond the projected December 15, 1950, deadline. McGrath concurred in the proposal that the commission consist of five members due to the proposed breadth of its duties.[10]

On June 3, 1950, Truman, through Executive Order 10129, established a five-member President's Commission on Migratory Labor to investigate the following areas of migrant labor:

First, the social, economic, health and educational conditions among migratory workers in the United States, and responsibilities now being assumed by federal, state, county and municipal authorities to alleviate conditions among these workers.

Second, the problems created by the migration into the United States of alien workers for temporary employment, and the extent to which alien workers were currently required to supplement the domestic labor supply.

Third, the extent of illegal migration of foreign workers into the United States, and whether and how law enforcement measures might be improved to eliminate illegal migration.[11]

In a statement accompanying Executive Order 10129 the President explained that estimates of the total number of migratory workers had varied between one and five million, and that previous studies had demonstrated migrant working conditions were far below those of other elements of the working population because migrants were denied the benefits of federal, state or local social legislation.[12]

The White House statement acknowledged that many organizations had voiced their opposition to further alien labor importation, contending that domestic labor was sufficient, while other groups insisted that adequate farm production required a seasonal supply of alien agricultural labor.[13]

The National Farm Labor Union credited itself with the decision to establish a Commission on Migratory Labor. Henry L. Mitchell, NFLU President, in citing support from California Representatives Helen Gahagan Douglas and John F. Shelley; from William Green, President of the American Federation of Labor; and from the NAACP, declared that the Commission resulted in great part from his union's campaign "to alert the public to the menace of illegal alien labor to American agricultural workers."[14]

Executive Order 10129 provided for a chairman and four other members to be designated by the President. Several interest groups lobbied intensively to place one of their members on the Commission. Walter White, Secretary of the NAACP, requested from Truman that he select a black member because "so large a percentage of migratory workers are colored."[15] Religious organizations such as the Detroit Council of Churches also urged the appointment of a black as well as a member of the religious community.[16] F. D. Patterson, President of Tuskegee Institute, recommended Claude Albert Barnett. Barnett had received an Honorary Doctorate of Humanities from Tuskegee, since 1938 had served as Special Assistant to the Secretary of Agriculture, was a member of the President's Committee for the Physically Handicapped, and had founded the Associated Negro Press in 1919.[17] He was not appointed.

Senator Edwin C. Johnson, Chairman of the Senate Committee on Interstate and Foreign Commerce, lobbied in behalf of one of his constituents who wanted the Commission to include someone who had lived and worked directly with the Mexican migrant and possessed the same ethnic and social background.[18]

Union groups, which had previously lobbied unsuccessfully to obtain a voice in the decision-making process which drew up international farm worker agreements to certify the need for Mexican labor or to establish the employer-determined prevailing wage, also requested representation on the Commission. Jacob Potofsky, President of the Amalgamated Clothing Workers of America, was one of many labor leaders who requested union membership.[19]

Some noteworthy individuals from the legal, educational, religious, political and Mexican-American communities were under consideration as prospective Commission members, including Robert M. LaFollette, former Senator of Wisconsin; Harold Ickes, former Secretary of the Interior; David Chavez, United States District Judge in San Juan, Puerto Rico; Mildred McAfee Horton, President of Wellesley College; George Sanchez, Professor of Latin American Education at the University of Texas; Theodore Shultz of the Department of Economics at the University of Chicago; William Myers, a conservative professor at the New York State School of Agriculture, who would be acceptable to the growers and the conservative Farm Bureau; Knowles A. Ryerson, Assistant Dean of the College of Agriculture and Coordinator of Veterans Affairs at the University of California, Davis; Jonathan Daniels, Truman's former press secretary, 1945, and editor of the Raleigh News and Observer; Most Reverend Robert E. Lucey, Archbishop of San Antonio; and Right Reverend Monsignor Liggutti, of the National Catholic Rural Life Conference.[20]

Others received support for membership to the President's Commission on Migratory Labor. Senator Lyndon Baines Johnson of Texas recommended a Tom Sutherland.[21] The Bureau of the Budget suggested Nelson Rockefeller, Coordinator of Inter-American Affairs, 1940-1945; Congressman William L. Dawson recommended Thomas E. Posey of West Virginia State College; Dorothy Smith McAllister of the Women's Democratic Club, International Social Service, was the choice of the Labor Department as was Murray Lincoln, President and Director of the Cooperative League of the United States.[22]

In the end, Truman appointed a Chairman, four Commissioners and an Executive Secretary with impressive credentials. The Chairman was Maurice T. Van Hecke, Professor of Law at the University of North Carolina, who had been Chairman of

Region 4 of the National War Labor Board, 1942-1945. The four other members were Archbishop Robert E. Lucey, Chairman of the Bishops' Committee for the Spanish Speaking People of the Southwest; William M. Leiserson, labor disputes arbitrator, who had been president, in 1951, of the Industrial Relations Research Association, was former Chairman of the National Mediation Board, and was a former member of the National Labor Relations Board; Peter H. Odegard, Chairman of the Department of Political Science at the University of California and President, in 1951, of the American Political Science Association; and Paul Miller, Chief of the University of Minnesota Extension Service. When Miller resigned after a few weeks of service, Truman replaced him with Noble Clark, Associate Director of the Agricultural Experiment Station of the University of Wisconsin and Former Deputy Director General of the Food and Agricultural Organization of the United Nations.[23] Varden Fuller, Agricultural Economist for the Giannini Foundation and the Agricultural Experiment Station at the University of California, was named Executive Secretary.[24]

The Commission contained one lawyer, one clergyman, one political scientist, one labor mediator, one economist and one agriculture expert. Four of the six were scholars from the academic community. Truman did not appoint any blacks, women or representatives of organized labor.[25] Assistant Secretary of Labor Gibson echoed the sentiments of administration officials who felt that if labor had representation on the committee, the employer groups would demand the same. The result, according to Gibson, would be the issuance of several minority reports.[26] The body of a commission should represent those groups under study, even at the risk of sacrificing unanimity. Although a series of minority reports might not be as pleasing to an administration as a unanimous recommendation, the former would at least reflect the divergence of opinion over highly complex issues. Gibson had misconstrued the nature of a commission.

The inevitable protests were levied at the administration when the Commissioners were announced.[27] Ernst Schwarz, Executive Secretary of the Congress of Industrial Organization's Committee on Latin American Affairs, expressed bewilderment that a Commission designed to investigate labor problems would operate without labor representation.[28]

At the Washington hearings, Clarence Mitchell, Labor Secretary of the NAACP, expressed dissatisfaction with the all-white Migratory Labor Commission.[29] Mitchell indicted the government and the Commission:

> The exclusion of them (blacks) from membership of this committee shows that the United States Department of Labor and the Department of Agriculture are either unaware of or indifferent to the stake that we have in the problems which this committee is set up to study. We hope that one of the first official actions taken by the committee will be a recommendation to the President that a qualified colored member be appointed.[30]

Except for Clark's replacement for Miller, the President did not alter or expand the Commission membership.

The President's Commission on Migratory Labor was a product of an executive order without Congressional initiative or approval. It could be financed only through executive funding such as the "Emergency Fund for the President" appropriation in the Independent Offices Appropriation Act of 1950 (Public Law 266), approved August 24, 1949. For fiscal year 1951, it was funded again through a new appropriation for the President's Emergency Fund.[31]

The Commission used three methods of information-gathering in compiling its final report--hearings, field trips and conferences. The hearings were conducted nationwide with twelve public hearings in Brownsville, Texas; El Paso, Texas; Phoenix, Arizona; Los Angeles, California; Portland, Oregon; Fort Collins, Colorado; Memphis, Tennessee; Saginaw, Michigan; Trenton, New Jersey, West Palm Beach, Florida; and two in Washington, D.C. Each of the twelve hearings was regional in coverage and received testimony from labor unions, farmers, employers, growers and processors. In addition, federal, state and local government officials, social workers, public health officials, religious groups, educational spokesmen, and migrant workers appeared at these hearings.[32] In connection with most of the hearings, the Commission made field trips to communicate with workers and employers in order to observe actual working conditions.

In addition to holding two Washington hearings, the Commission held two conferences in that city to obtain testimony from government agencies, including the Departments of Labor, State and Agriculture, the Immigration and Naturalization Service, and the Federal Security Agency. The first conference, In June, 1950, was held to enable the above-named agencies to brief the Commission on the problems incident to migratory labor. The second conference was conducted in November to discuss specific recommendations of these agencies.[33]

The President's Commission on Migratory Labor also conducted conferences with state agency officials of California, Colorado, New Jersey, and New York; with representatives of the Government of Mexico and the territory of Puerto Rico; and with State Agricultural Extension Services and the American Farm Economic Association. Furthermore, some Commission members held observer status at a conference between the Department of State and representatives of the Government of the British West Indies; at a conference and a hearing which the Farm Labor Subcommittee of the House Agriculture Committee sponsored; and at a conference of the Advisory Council of the United States Employment Service.[34]

Labor representatives were articulate spokesmen at the nationwide hearings. In summing up the criticism and recommendations of labor, William Green told the Commission that the importation of foreign labor had denied employment to the most underprivileged labor group in the United States. Green recommended:

First: Labor organizations of farm workers in both this country and in Mexico should be given full status in a consultant capacity whenever international agreements providing for importation of farm workers are considered.

Second: Hearings should be held ... before a finding is made that there is a shortage requiring importation of foreign workers. The actual investigation should be made by a tripartite board in which employers, workers and the government are represented.

Third: Aliens should be guaranteed a minimum wage of 75 cents

an hour and contracts should permit the alien workers to join American labor organizations for the
period during which they were employed in this country.[35]

Green also advocated strengthening the I and NS to impede the entrance of wetbacks
into the United States.

Labor attacked the agribusiness rejoinder that domestic labor simply refused or was unable to do "stoop" and other arduous types of farm labor.[36] Labor
unions criticized grower organizations for neglecting to mention that low wages and
dismal working conditions were also a hindrance in securing an adequate domestic
farm labor supply.[37] Labor further urged the Commission to recommend the adoption
of legislation which penalized the unlawful employment of non-contract Mexican
labor.[38]

Another common labor complaint dealt with migratory labor's working and
living conditions. H. L. Mitchell testified that not since the wartime labor program direction of the Farm Security Administration had there been attempts to re-
habilitate low-income farm families and control agribusiness abuse of the worker.[39]
Bernard Valdez, of the Colorado Migrant Labor Council, told the Commission at the
Fort Collins, Colorado, hearings that since the demise of the Farm Security Administration, rents for migrants had increased 400% while actual migrant housing conditions decreased in quality.[40]

Agribusiness interests also appeared at these Commission hearings throughout the nation.   Keith Mets, President of the powerful Imperial Valley Farmers'
Association, which consisted of approximately 500 wealthy California farmers, presented the growers' position in testimony at Los Angeles on August 12, 1950.[41]

Since most of the alien labor demand occurred during the fall harvest
season, Mets advocated that work contracts be shortened from several months to
four to eight weeks.[42] Mets attempted to discredit the NFLU by requesting that
the USES withdraw its ruling that prior to certification of a domestic farm labor
shortage, the NFLU be granted a thirty-day period to supply domestic workers. The
powerful grower cited Congressman Richard Nixon's House Agricultural Subcommittee
report that the NFLU had lied about the existence of quasi-feudal conditions on
the Joseph DiGiorgio ranch as proof that the NFLU should be disqualified from parti-
cipating in the bracero program.[43] Mets wanted the Department of Agriculture and
its extension services to assume migratory labor functions of the Department of
Labor and USES.

The Imperial Valley Farmers' Association advocated the establishment of
a border-crossing card system (white card) enabling a free flow of Mexican labor
with a minimum of regulations and red tape. To guarantee the continuance of a
cheap migratory labor supply, another grower suggestion was to legislate an alien
labor program without a termination date.[44]

The Department of State was one of many government departments to appear
at the Second General Conference at Washington, D.C., on November 6-7, 1950.[45]
The State Department suggested the formation of a permanent Joint United States-

Mexican Labor Commission in which the President would appoint a United States Commissioner, to be located at El Paso, Texas, who would be responsible to the State Department. The Commissioner would have advisers from the United States Employment Service and the Immigration and Naturalization Service to help administer the bracero program. Evelyn Randall, Secretary to Chairman Van Hecke, who frequently made comments on testimony, criticized the State Department's suggestion of becoming involved in the domestic functions of certifying and recruitment as "amounting to little more than an extension into the field of a State Department Activity".[46] She also reacted cynically to State's prediction that, in the event of an insufficient Mexican labor supply, agribusiness would conduct a labor hunt into the Central American nations of Guatemala and Costa Rica; "Would there then have to be joint commissions with each and every such supply source?"[47]

The State Department envisioned this Joint Commission as a device to streamline the certification and recruitment process. As it existed, the certification process dealt with many agencies beginning with the State Labor Commissions, going to the USES, then to the Mexican Foreign Office, and finally back to the contracting center. Under State Department proposal, the Joint Commission would conduct on-the-spot recruitment and certification, thereby resulting in an efficiently operated program:

> (Even the)congestion of braceros at Mexican border towns,
> which is now of great concern to the Mexican Government,
> could be avoided and full consideration could be given to
> Mexico's desire to assure itself of sufficient labor before
> any Mexicans work on United States farms.[48]

The Department of State reiterated its long-standing opposition to border recruitment by reporting that due to an increase in Mexican agricultural activity in Baja California, in the Mexican states of Sinaloa and Sonora, and in the cotton areas of the Reynosa-Matzatlan triangle, the demand for its own farm laborers in northern Mexico was great. State felt that border recruitment would prove injurious to Mexico's farm needs.

The State Department suggested that the Commission visualize the Mexican bracero crisis in terms of its being an important thread in the total fabric of Mexican-United States relations and not in the narrow framework of a domestic dispute between unions and employers.

The Department of Labor, which was responsible for certifying and recruiting Mexican labor, offered its views at Commission conferences in Washington.[49] The Labor Department believed the nation's economy "demands" the migration of huge supplies of migrant labor in order to meet seasonal production requirements. But the demand for a foreign labor component would be diminished if domestic labor were provided with greater work incentives. These incentives, according to labor, should include the uplifting of domestic agricultural working conditions which the agribusiness industry and the absence of federal farm labor legislation denied them. In any event, binational agreements should not continue to guarantee minimum working conditions for aliens which domestic labor was not receiving.

The Department of Labor recommended that foreign recruitment be suspended except in cases of national emergency. Labor agreed with the unions that wetbacks should be eliminated and strong punitive anti-wetback legislation be enacted. However, Varden Fuller, Executive Secretary of the President's Commission on Migratory Labor, was critical of the generalities of Labor's recommendations. He specifically took exception to the lack of concrete proposals dealing with the specific provisions of punitive legislation or the enforcement of such a law.[50]

At the Phoenix hearings on August 7 and August 8, 1950, O. W. Manney, Phoenix Chief of the Immigration Service, Carson Morrow, Arizona Chief Border Patrol Inspector at Tucson, and Fred N. Thomas, Border Patrol Chief at Phoenix, testified that a powerful group of agribusiness interests was compelling the suspension of law enforcement against wetbacks in order to receive cheap labor. Morrow testified that he received orders from the District Director at El Paso each harvest to stop deporting illegal Mexican labor. Manney asserted that importation on grounds of necessity had been abused to the extent that there was "a year around emergency". [51]

It was becoming apparent that the extent of the hearings and the necessity to present a report on both domestic and alien migratory labor would preclude the submission of the report on December 15, 1950. Truman, at the urging of the Commission, decided that a new executive order was warranted. The drafting of this second migratory labor executive order took place in the Budget Bureau, with its revision being handled in the Justice Department.[52] Executive Order 10192 was promulgated on December 15, 1950; it extended the deadline for the final report to March 1, 1951, and provided for the dissolution of the Commission sixty days after it submitted its report. The previous executive order provided for a thirty-day period.

On March 26, 1951, having been allowed a further deadline by Executive Order 10236, the Commission completed its final report and gave it to the President.[53] The resultant news release did not occur until April 7, 1951. It is interesting to note the background of such an announcement. Chairman Van Hecke wanted the hometown newspapers of the Commission members and Executive Secretary to be provided with leaks that the announcement of the Commission's final report was imminent. The Commission informed Joseph Short, Truman's Press Secretary from 1950-1952, who was responsible for handling such a news release, that it would prefer to avoid a press conference, letting the report speak for itself. Van Hecke suggested the press release include a picture of the President and his Commission on Migratory Labor.[54]

The Commission's recommendations were essentially pro-labor and anti-agribusiness. It called for a tightening of border patrol enforcement and the elimination of illegal forms of labor entry. The report supported organized labor's demands for legislation making it unlawful to employ non-contract Mexicans and advocated the elimination of the previous practice of legalizing wetbacks.

The final report condemned the USES as operating under a conflict of interest because it had the dual responsibility of certifying domestic labor shortages and providing labor for the farm industry:

When the agency which certifies a labor shortage is also the agency which fills that shortage by importation, it is much too easy to offset an ineffective recruitment and placement job at home by importing workers from abroad.[55]

The final report advocated sweeping administrative reorganization in which the I and NS would become the principal agency in administering "foreign-labor recruiting, contracting, transportation and agreements". After the USES certified the need for foreign workers, it would be stripped of any administrative function with regard to the bracero program. The I and NS should deliver the imported workers to United States farms, guarantee their conditions of employment, remove any worker if compelled to do so and prevent any farm or grower association from further hiring of contract labor if the former violated intergovernmental agreements.[56]

Another major administrative reform was the proposed creation of a Federal Committee on Migratory Labor. This Committee would have eight members appointed by the President: three public members and one each from the Department of Agriculture, Department of Labor, Department of State, I and NS, and the Federal Security Agency. Although the Federal Committee on Migratory Labor would have no administrative or permanent operating responsibilities, its purpose would be to mediate and coordinate the activites of federal agencies dealing with migratory labor.[57] The final report advocated the development of similar State Committees on Migratory Labor to rationalize state administration of migrancy and to complement the activities of the Federal Committee on Migratory Labor.[58]

Because the commission was a progressive one, the call for structural and administrative change was not surprising. While the centralization of services into the I and NS was the result of the input of many groups testifying before the commission, the Federal Committee on Migratory Labor was not. The latter proposal seemed to create bureaucratic zones of indecision. If the I and NS was to have seemingly exclusive power in running the binational labor program, why would it have only one representative on the Federal Committee? If it were to have no administrative or enforcement power, could it be expected to preside effectively over an inoperative migratory labor program? The Committee was to have authority to establish advisory committees. Would not this proliferation of administrative and advisory departments vitiate the Commission's own reform-minded attempts at simplifying the administrative structure?

Government agency reaction to the report was mixed. The Bureau of Employment Security, a division within the Department of Labor which included the USES, was outraged by the Migratory Labor Report. The Bureau accused the President's Commission on Migratory Labor of bias, inaccurate and inconsistent statements, misleading references, and a total lack of understanding of USES migrant labor policies and practices.[59] Robert C. Goodwin, formerly the Director of the USES and promoted to Bureau Chief of Employment Security, defended the USES from the charge of maintaining a close relationship with employers by asserting this was necessary to maintain an efficient recruitment of foreign workers. Goodwin did not deny an additional charge that in some instances the USES designated an employer as the sole recruiting agent in Mexico.

Goodwin responded to the accusation that the Farm Placement Service of the USES placed greater emphasis on its function as a recruiter for employers than on its equally important function as a work-finding agency for domestic migrants, by stating that the Farm Placement Service was not the sole medium through which all migratory workers found employment and that it should not be blamed for problems in this area.[60]

This study has pointed out many abuses of the USES with regard to its hard-line approach to negotiations with Mexico, its obsession with encouraging indiscriminate Mexican immigration as exemplified by the El Paso Incident, and its general reluctance to recruit exhaustively domestic labor prior to certifying the necessity for foreign recruitment. The USES was an easy target for the Commission. When the Imperial Valley Farmers Association told the Commission that the USES was anathema to "the American farmer in the entire Southwest", because it was an agency of the Department of Labor and had made feeble attempts to include labor as a voice in the certification process, the USES had lost its staunchest ally.[61]

Truman received direct evaluation of the Commission report from Attorney General McGrath.[62] McGrath's Justice Department contained I and NS, which was to administer the labor program. McGrath wrote Truman that the I and NS was ill-suited for such an enlargement of duties because it lacked expertise in personnel and had insufficient funding. The I and NS, McGrath explained, was a law enforcement agency which was not geared to rectify the problems of employment service, farm service or labor relations which other government agencies handled.

McGrath favored wholeheartedly the Commission recommendations that domestic labor be given hiring preference and that the I and NS be made more effective in preventing the violation of immigration laws. The Attorney General elaborated upon the report's provision for increased I and NS appropriations for personnel and equipment by requesting 864 additional border patrol inspectors, two detention camps (each of which could hold 1500 Mexicans waiting to be deported), and immediate funds to remove to the Mexican interior 116,000 illegal itinerant workers.[63]

Union sentiment was favorable despite labor's exclusion from Commission membership. James G. Patton, President of the liberal Farmers Union, praised Truman and the Commission for raising the national level of consciousness to the point where migratory labor conditions received the investigation of a Commission.[64] The AF of L's William Green was "favorabley impressed" with the Commission on Migratory Labor's final report.[65] Even H. L. Mitchell, the most strident union critic of the bracero program, was satisfied with the findings and recommendations of the Commission and urged the quick adoption of the proposed Committee on Migratory Labor.[66] The NFLU National Representative, William Becker, reflected labor's attitude, declaring that the final report had given him new hope in the government's determination to improve the condition of migratory labor.[67] This unanimity of praise reflected the Commission's preoccupation at devising means of hiring domestic labor and preventing continued abuse of migratory labor, be it foreign or domestic.

President Truman desired further reaction to the report and institutionalized broad administrative feedback. Between the completion of the report and its release to the public, copies were sent to the Departments of Agriculture, State, Labor, Justice and Interior, the Federal Security Agency and the Housing and Home

Finance Administrator for their comment. The Bureau of the Budget created a Special Task Force to issue its own report synthesizing agency comment and offering its own reaction to the Commission's final report.68

The Task Force Report was completed on July 12, 1951, but not submitted until January, 1952.69 Both the Budget Bureau Task Force and the Agencies agreed that foreign labor importation must be conducted under the terms of inter-governmental agreement. The Federal Security Agency and the Department of Labor questioned the desirability of an agreement which would insure better standards for Mexican workers than for United States workers.70

The Commission on Migratory Labor recommended that international agreements promote the enforcement of immigration laws and serve as the exclusive vehicle for the importation of contract Mexican braceros. Agencies generally favored these recommendations but were skeptical of Mexico's ability to prevent the emigration of its workers. Agency comment tended to emphasize only the "push" forces as contributing to wetback invasion, i.e., the economic differential between Mexico and the United States; Mexican overpopulation; Mexican inflation and the inability of Mexican agriculture to absorb its native farm working sector. The Task Force advocated continued efforts by the Departments of State and Labor to strengthen the international agreement and the coordination of the efforts of United States immigration officials with those of the Mexican Government to end illegal immigration of farm workers.71

The Budget Bureau Special Task Force concurred with the principle of massive structural reorganization but not the process. The Task Force was critical of the USES practice of allowing farmers to hire Mexicans on their own and desired a separation of the domestic labor program from the alien, but did not support replacement of the USES by the I and NS. Both the Agencies and the Task Force, while agreeing with the recommendation that the foreign labor importation program be placed in one agency, basically advocated the status quo. The Task Force called for an all-powerful Foreign Labor Unit within the Farm Placement Service of the USES of the Bureau of Employment Security of the Department of Labor to run the program. It should be stressed again that the Bureau of Employment Security was under the direction of Goodwin. Obviously, his agency, USES, which had been accused of illegal and incompetent performance, could not be expected to reform itself radically and produce the type of administration that the Commission and the unions desired.

Far from desiring the diminution of USES activity, the Task Force actually suggested an increase in USES duties which the Commission withheld from its all-powerful agency, the I and NS. This area was foreign affairs. The Task Force wanted the USES to assume the diplomatic chores of the State Department in areas dealing with the binational labor program; specifically, it wanted the Foreign Labor Unit of the Farm Placement Service to be the decisive agency in negotiating international agreements.72 Even the Commission's proposed centralization of administration excluded the abandonment of the State Department's function in drawing up binational agreements.73

The President's Commission on Migratory Labor, the Budget Bureau Task Force and the Government Agencies voiced their opposition to wetback labor. The

Commission offered the following reforms in this critical area:

> (1)   I and NS be strengthened by (a) clear statutory auth-
> ority to enter places of employment to determine if illegal
> aliens are employed, (b) clear statutory penalties for har-
> boring, concealing or transporting illegal aliens...
> (2)   Legislation be enacted making it unlawful to employ aliens
> illegally in the United States, the sanctions to be (a) remov-
> al by the I and NS of all legally imported labor from any
> place of employment on which any illegal alien is found em-
> ployed; (b) fine and imprisonment; (c) restraining orders and
> injunctions and (d) prohibiting the shipment in interstate
> commerce of any product on which illegal alien labor has
> worked.
> (3)   Legislation for employment purposes of aliens illegally
> in the United States be discontinued and forbidden...
> (4)   The Department of State seek the active cooperation of
> ... Mexico in ... (a) strict enforcement of the Mexican emi-
> gration laws, (b) preventing the concentration, in areas close
> to the border, of surplus supplies of Mexican labor...[74]

The reaction in principle to these anti-wetback provisions was favorable. Justice favored less forceful punitive legislation without the sanctions
of restraining orders, injunctions and bans of the interstate commerce of wetback
products. The Departments of Labor and State agreed that the legalization of wetbacks was counterproductive. The Task Force remarked that wetback legalization
"makes a mockery of the immigration laws and tends to break down the whole enforcement program."[75]

There appeared to be, however, skepticism that the immigration laws could
be enforced and that punitive Congressional legislation could be enacted. McGrath
informed Truman that "immigration law enforcement ... will not keep that surplus
labor ... from eventually spilling over into our border." McGrath, instead of at-
tributing agribusiness "pull" forces as a cause of wetbacks, attributed the "push"
forces of the Mexican economy as causing a starving desperate bloc of impoverished
Mexican farm workers seeking admission into the United States.[76] The Task Force
also concluded that without a virtual overhauling of the Mexican economy, the invasion would continue regardless of whether the Commission report became administration policy or not. The Budget Bureau advocated the specific application of
Truman's Point IV Program of assistance to developing nations to Mexico as a means
of eliminating the "push" forces causing excessive Mexican labor in the United
States.

Throughout the existence of this labor program, it has been demonstrated
that the attitude of farmers was that they were entitled to Mexican farm labor on
a regular seasonal basis. This sentiment was a major "pull" force which contributed
to illegal border crossings. The United States initiated the concept of legalizing
wetbacks which was a signal to any aspiring immigrant from Mexico that if he initially entered the United States illegally, he would eventually become a legalized
worker. The Commission report left no doubt of its assessment: "The United States
...has encouraged violation of the immigration laws. Our Government thus has

become a contributor to the growth of an illegal traffic which it has responsibility to prevent."[77]

The Commission approached the emotion-laden issue of bracero labor with probity and detachment as its excellent study into the history of the Mexican war worker program during the 1940s up to mid-1950 demonstrated. But its recommendations failed to generate concrete reform, although they were publicly praised by the President and prominent Congressmen. Subsequent administrations ignored these proposals with the result being a total breakdown in binational governance of the labor program.

Footnotes:

1. Roy Wilkins to the President, October 10, 1949, OF 407-D, Truman Papers, Truman Library.

2. John W. Gibson to Carl D. Davenport, March 24, 1950, Migratory Labor 1950 Folder, Department of Labor, Assistant Secretary John W. Gibson (RG 174), National Archives.

3. Harry S. Truman to Norman Thomas, November 5, 1949, OF 407-D, Truman Papers, Truman Library; Harry S. Truman to Roy Wilkins, November 8, 1949, OF 407-D, Truman Papers, Truman Library.

4. Truman to Thomas, November 5, 1949.

5. Truman to Wilkins, November 8, 1949.

6. Ibid.

7. Harry S. Truman to Helen Gahagan Douglas, November 5, 1949, OF 407-D, Truman Papers, Truman Library; Harry S. Truman to H. L. Mitchell, November 5, 1949, OF 407-D, Truman Papers, Truman Library.

8. Maurice J. Tobin to the President, February 27, 1950, OF 407-E, Truman Papers, Truman Library.

9. Ibid.

10. J. Howard McGrath to Frederick J. Lawton, May 4, 1950, OF 407-E, Truman Papers, Truman Library. Assistant Director of the Budget Bureau Roger W. Jones circulated copies of the executive order to enlist the comments of various departments. Although McGrath failed to stop or delimit the scope of the executive order, future extensions of the submission of the report were granted in recognition of the enormity of the Commission's task.

11. The Department of State Bulletin, July 3, 1950, p. 33; New York Times, June 4, 1940 (hereafter referred to as NYT).

12. "President Names Commission to Study Migratory Labor Problems", U. S. Department of Labor Press Release, Week of June 12, 1950, Migratory Labor 1950 Folder, Department of Labor, Office of the Secretary (RG 174), National Archives; NYT, June 4, 1950.

13. "President Names Commission", Labor Press Release.

14. NYT, June 4, 1950.

15. Telegram, Walter White to the President, June 30, 1950, OF 407-E, Truman Papers, Truman Library.

16. G. Merrill Lenox to the President, June 22, 1950, OF 407-E, Truman Papers, Truman Library.

17. F. D. Patterson to the President, June 14, 1950, OF 407-E, Truman Papers, Truman Library.

18. Edwin C. Johnson to the President, June 19, 1950, OF 407-E, Truman Papers, Truman Library.

19. Jacob Potofsky to John W. Gibson, March 21, 1950, Migratory Labor 1950 Folder, Department of Labor, Assistant Secretary, John W. Gibson (RG 174), National Archives.

20. "Prospects for President's Committee on Migratory Labor", Department of Labor, Office of the Secretary, Assistant Secretary Robert T. Creasey (RG 174), National Archives. This list was marked, "Confidential". Except for Van Hecke, the Department of Labor was the originator of all these candidates, with other agencies concurring. The Federal Security Agency (Myers, Shultz, Lucey, Sanchez), the Department of State (Horton), the Department of Agriculture (Liggutti), Bureau of the Budget (Van Hecke) and Philleo Nash (Sanchez).

21. Donald S. Dawson to Lyndon Baines Johnson, June 22, 1950, OF 407-E, Truman Papers, Truman Library.

22. William L. Dawson to Charles F. Brannan, March 2, 1950, Migratory Labor 1950 Folder, Department of Labor, Assistant Secretary John W. Gibson (RG 174), National Archives; "Prospects for Committee"; "Persons Suggested for Membership on President's Commission on Migratory Labor", OF 407-E, Truman Papers, Truman Library.

23. Matthew J. Connelly to the President, July 5, 1950, OF 407-E, Truman Papers, Truman Library.

24. Memorandum, Evelyn S. Randall, to Joseph Short, April 2, 1951, Administration File Folder, Records of the President's Commission on Migratory Labor, Truman Library. Special assistance was also given to the Commission by experts on loan from the Farm Home Administration, the Bureau of Agricultural Economics, the Immigration and Naturalization Service, the Bureau of Labor Standards, the United States Employment Service, the Wage and Hour Division, the California State Department of Industrial Relations and the University of California. See: Monthly Labor Review, United States Department of Labor, Bureau of Labor Statistics, June 1951, p. 693. Full-time staff members, in addition to Executive Secretary Fuller and Secretary to the Chairman Randall were: Harold E. Benson, Barbara J. Berglund, Max A. Egloff, Jerry G. Foreman, Seymour G. Gresser, Eleanor M. Hadley, Florence A. Irle, Robert C. Jones, Samuel Liss (on full-time loan from the Farm Home Administration), Edwin C. Pendleton and William C. Porter.

25. Although women were on some preliminary lists, there were none with black or labor representatives being considered for appointment. Even when Miller resigned, attempts of black groups to get serious consideration for the appointment of a black failed.

26. Potofsky to Gibson, March 21, 1950.

27. The members themselves were not criticized for their credentials were substantial; the criticism was directed at the general exclusion of blacks and union spokesmen.

28. Ernst Schwartz to Commission, July 13-14, 1950, Washington D. C. Hearings, Records of the President's Commission on Migratory Labor, Truman Library.

29. Clarence Mitchell to Commission, July 13, 1950, Washington D.C. Hearings, Records of the President's Commission on Migratory Labor, Truman Library.

30. Ibid.

31. Harry S. Truman to Maurice T. Van Hecke, October 11, 1950; April 23, 1951; May 16, 1951, OF 407-E, Truman Papers, Truman Library; Harry S. Truman to John W. Snyder, June 3, 1950; July 13, 1950; August 2, 1950, OF 407-E, Truman Papers, Truman Library; The Department of State Bulletin, July 3, 1950, p. 33.

32. Randall to Short, April 2, 1951; U. S. Department of Labor Press Release, Week of July 24, 1950, Migratory Labor 1950 Folder, Department of Labor, Office of the Secretary (RG 174), National Archives.

33. Records of second General Conference, Washington, D.C., November 6-7, 1950, Records of the President's Commission on Migratory Labor, Truman Library.

34. Randall to Short, April 2, 1951.

35. William Green to Maurice T. Van Hecke, October 26, 1950, Correspondence: Migratory Labor August 15-February 23, 1951, Folder, Records of the President's Commission on Migratory Labor. Truman Library. See also, F. R. Betton, undated, Memphis, Tennessee, August 31-September 1, 1950 Statements Folder, Records of the President's Commission on Migratory Labor, Truman Library.

36. NYT, August 13, 1950. Peter Odegard became irritated at suggestions that United States labor was incapable of performing arduous farm labor. See NYT, September 7, 1950; State Farm Labor Placement Service Officials claimed in addition to the growers that United States labor could not or would not perform rigorous "stoop" labor or fruit picking tasks. See: NYT, August 11, 1950.

37. NYT, August 13, 1950.

38. NYT, September 7, 1950.

39. H. L. Mitchell to Commission, August 31-September 1, 1950, Memphis, Tennessee, Statements Folder, President's Commission on Migratory Labor, Truman Library.

40. Bernard Valdez to Commission, Fort Collins, Colorado, August 17-18, 1950, Statements Folder, Records of the President's Commission on Migratory Labor, Truman Library.

41. Keith Mets to Commission, Los Angeles, California, August 10-12, 1950, Statements Folder, Records of the President's Commission on Migratory Labor, Truman Library. For another typical grower's statement see: E. S. McSweeney, Executive Secretary, Arizona Cooperative Cotton Growers Association, to Commission, Phoenix, Arizona, August 7-8, 1950, Statement Folder, Records of the President's Commission on Migratory Labor, Truman Library.

42. Although amendments to Article 12 of the 1949 Mexican-United States Agreement provided for six-week seasonal contracts in the lower Rio Grande Valley, these were the exception. Mets wanted seasonal contracting for all areas. It is important to understand that most farmers did not want a permanent supply of Mexican labor in the United States. Due to increasing mechanization and the seasonal nature of fruit and vegetable farming, a big supply of labor was needed for only a few months each fall. Farm employers were primarily concerned about the uncertainty and unreliability of their seasonal labor supply and wanted guarantees of having such labor when they desired it.

43. NYT, August 13, 1950.

44. Mets to Commission, August 10-12, 1950; See also La Monte Graw, Manager of the Florida Fruit and Vegetable Association, to Commission, at Washington Hearing, July 15, 1950, Department of Labor Press Release, Week of July 24, 1950.

45. "Recommendations of the Department of State", Records of Second General Conference, Washington, D.C., November 6-7, 1950, Records of the President's Commission on Migratory Labor, Truman Library.

46. Evelyn Randall to Maurice T. Van Hecke, Records of Second General Conference, Washington, D.C., November 6-7, 1950, Records of the President's Commission on Migratory Labor, Truman Library.

47. Ibid.

48. Ibid.

49. Suggested Recommendations of the United States Department of Labor to the President's Commission on Migratory Labor, October 1950, Commission on Migratory Labor (President's) Folder, Department of Labor, Office of the Secretary, Assistant Secretary Creasey (RG 174), National Archives.

50. Notes: Varden Fuller, November 7, 1950, Records of the Second General Conference, Washington, D.C., November 6-7, 1950, Records of the President's Commission on Migratory Labor, Truman Library.

51. NYT, August 9, 1950.

52. Peyton Ford to the President, December 12, 1950, Records OF 407-E, Truman Papers, Truman Library. The first executive order 10129 was drafted in Justice and revised by the Budget Bureau.

53. Report of the President's Commission on Migratory Labor, Migratory Labor in American Agriculture, 1951.

54. Randall to Short, April 2, 1951.

55. Migratory Labor Report, p. 62.

56. Ibid., pp. 66-67.

57. Noble Clark, William M. Leiserson, Robert E. Lucey, Peter H. Odegard, Maurice T. Van Hecke to the President, March 26, 1951, Records of the President's Commission on Migratory Labor, Truman Library; Ibid.

58. Clark et al, to the President, March 26, 1951; Migratory Labor Report, pp. 177-178.

59. Robert C. Goodwin to Maurice J. Tobin, August 9, 1951, Employment Security 1951 Folder, Department of Labor, Office of the Secretary, Secretary Maurice Tobin, National Archives.

60. Ibid.

61. Mets to Commission, August 10-12, 1950.

62. J. Howard McGrath to the President, June 5, 1951, The President, Attorney General Desk Correspondence Folder, McGrath Papers, Truman Library.

63. Ibid.; Migratory Labor Report, p. 88.

64. James G. Patton to the President, April 11, 1951, OF 407-E, Truman Papers, Truman Library.

65. William Green to the President, April 16, 1951, OF 407-E, Truman Papers, Truman Library.

66. H. L. Mitchell to the President, April 9, 1951, OF 407-E, Truman Papers, Truman Library.

67. William Becker to the President, April 24, 1951, OF 407-E, Truman Papers, Truman Library.

68. Memorandum, Harry S. Truman to Frederick J. Lawton, April 24, 1951, OF 407-E, Truman Papers, Truman Library. Truman did not initially seek the Department of Interior's views but added this agency to the list of those providing comment. See: Harry S. Truman to Maurice J. Tobin, April 24, 1951, OF 407-E, Truman Papers, Truman Library.

69. Memorandum, F. J. Lawton to the President, January 4, 1952, OF 407-E, Truman Papers, Truman Library; Interior was not mentioned as one of the agencies from which an opinion was solicited but, for the first time, a comment on the Commission report was sought from the National Labor Relations Board.

70. Task Force Report on Migratory Labor in Agriculture, Migratory Labor Folder, Stowe Papers, Truman Library; Suggested Recommendations of the U. S. Department of Labor to the President's Commission on Migratory Labor, October 1950, Records of the Second General Conference, Washington, D.C., November 6-7, 1950, Records of the President's Commission on Migratory Labor, Truman Library.

71. Task Force Report, p. 16.

72. Ibid., p. 21.

73. Migratory Labor Report, p.66.

74. Ibid., p. 180

75. Task Force Report, p. 24.

76. McGrath to the President, June 5, 1951.

77. Migratory Labor Report, pp. 74-75.

CHAPTER VII

AGRIBUSINESS, THE WETBACK AND THE FUTURE

The bracero program constituted one of the more controversial diplomatic programs in United States history. The Second World War provided the impetus for the creation of the program which was highlighted by diplomatic protest notes, abrogations and suspensions of international agreements, murder of Mexicans on the Rio Grande and conflict between domestic interest groups in a changing political-economic environment.

Although the binational environmental context for the creation of the farm and railroad labor programs was a wartime situation, the bracero program eventually fell under the aegis of subnational interest groups which were successful in prolonging the importation of contract Mexican labor into the postwar era. The farm program lasted until 1965, while the railroad labor component was terminated in 1946. These interest groups, which consisted primarily of agribusiness and to a lesser extent railroad companies, were able to alter the course of an intended wartime emergency measure into a long-term profitable program.

Agribusiness had strong allies in Congress and in several government agencies. During the 1940s, the Immigration and Naturalization Service, the United States Employment Service, the Border Patrol and the War Food Administration were prominent in their support of agribusiness' goal of a supply of inexpensive foreign farm labor. These agencies opted for a virtual open border allowing indiscriminate entry of any Mexican seeking work in the United States and lobbied intensively with Mexico to obtain border recruitment centers which would reduce grower recruitment costs and attract thousands of Mexican farm workers to the international border. These agencies, along with the Department of State, eliminated Mexico's practice of unilaterally blacklisting United States areas known for anti-Mexican discrimination from employing bracero labor.

The agribusiness industry further demonstrated its disdain for Mexican participation in the program and its ability to enlist the support of the United States Government by ignoring and subverting key provisions of the bracero intergovernmental agreements. These pacts, which provided the international legal framework for the bracero program, stipulated that no Mexican laborer could be imported until it was proven that a domestic labor shortage existed. This question of domestic labor availability to perform bracero tasks was one of the more hotly contested issues during the binational labor program. Both railway and farm labor unions adamantly insisted that United States labor was plentiful and willing to perform bracero tasks; they claimed that if a temporary labor shortage was present in a particular area, it could be attributed to below-subsistence wages and working conditions which were unacceptable to the American workingman. It became evident that agencies were certifying labor deficiencies when they did not exist. President Truman's Commission on Migratory Labor charged that the USES was wrongly assigned the task of certifying domestic labor shortages because the agency was prejudiced

102

in favor of agribusiness interests and thereby frequently compensated for its failure to recruit domestic labor by proclaiming that foreign labor was necessary to maintain adequate farm production.

With the introduction of the 1948 Mexican-United States Labor Agreement, the wetback was outlawed as both nations pledged to enforce strict border supervision. For years prior to 1948, Mexico had expressed concern over an uninhibited exodus of young, vigorous workers to the United States. Although Mexico was undoubtedly pleased that many thousands of its unemployed were acquiring work within the United States, the former expressed official concern over the depletion of a potentially productive component of its labor supply. Mexico fell prey to the power of organized American pressure groups.

Agribusiness also rebelled against internationally established working and living conditions for Mexican labor. Because there was an historic absence of social legislation protecting the domestic farm worker, farm employees had become accustomed to handling their employer-employee relations without governmental interference. The solution to preserving intact the traditional farmer-employee relationship without having to submit to internationally guaranteed work conditions was to hire illegal non-contract Mexican labor. These wetbacks were helpless in demanding minimum employment conditions on account of their illegal status which denied them protection under the international agreements. They had to fend for themselves, knowing that they might be repatriated if they protested their situation.

The recommendations of the Commission on Migratory Labor dealing with the elimination of the wetback were not implemented by subsequent administrations. Instead of securing the border and beefing up the Border Patrol, the United States in January 1954 instituted unilateral recruitment of Mexican labor without Mexico's consent.[1] This bold and arrogant policy was legislatively strengthened with the enactment of Public Law 309 (House Joint Resolution 355) on March 16, 1954, amending Public Law 78. Public Law 309 provided for the subversion of a bilateral labor program by allowing unilateral importation of foreign labor "after every practicable effort has been made by the United States to negotiate and reach agreement on such arrangements."[2]

This resulted in dramatic increases in Mexican national labor in the United States. Between 1954 and 1959, two and one-half million Mexicans were contracted with the greatest annual total of 445,197 arriving in 1956.[3] This 1956 total represents a greater number than the combined total of both the farm and railroad labor programs from 1942 to 1947.

The wetback was a major cause for the failure of the bracero program. An important question to raise was whether or not it was possible to cut the flow of wetbacks to a manageable level, and whether the wetback was mostly a product of United States governmental encouragement as well as economic desperation. A wall separating the two nations would have been effective in preventing emigration but politically and diplomatically prohibitive. A dramatic increase in border patrol funding and the passage of strictly enforced anti-wetback penalty legislation would have impeded the wetback invasion. Neither increases in border patrol funding or anti-wetback legislation became reality despite the Commission's recommendations. During the El Paso incident of October 1948, and again in 1954, the United States openly sought wetback immigration. From 1947 onwards, both nations legalized wetbacks already in the United States, which served to attract potential wetbacks who knew they would eventually become legal contract workers. The result was that farm interests with their Congressional and administration supporters defeated anti-bracero and anti-wetback forces for decades. Anti-braceroists included a congressional bloc consisting of Senators Paul Douglas, Wayne Morse, Eugene McCarthy, and Hubert Humphrey; such Representatives as George Stanley McGovern, Emmanuel Celler, John Shelley, Helen Gahagan Douglas and Howard Baker. The other unsuccessful anti-bracero group was farm unions, with the National Farm Labor Union being the most vocal and articulate.

The John F. Kennedy administration was responsible for the official termination of the binational bracero program. Kennedy's policy toward Latin America, with the exception of Cuba, attempted to overturn the Eisenhower-Dulles thrust of arrogance and unilateralism. From the United States' involvement in the overthrow of Guatemalan President Jacobo Arbenz in 1954 to the violent anti-American demonstrations against Vice-President Richard Nixon's tour of Peru and Venezuela in April, 1958, it was obvious that Eisenhower's Latin American policy had failed to defuse anti-United States fervor. Kennedy attempted to alter the previous unilateralism and substitute a foreign policy which was responsive to Latin American needs and desires. With regard to the bracero program, the new foreign policy entailed the recognition that Mexican labor was injurious to the United States farm worker and symbolic of United States aggressiveness toward Latin America. As Kennedy put it:

> The Mexican labor program ... is adversely affecting the wages, working conditions and employment opportunities of our own agricultural workers.[4]

In this same statement, however, Kennedy acknowledged the "push" forces in Mexico which created an unemployed, frustrated group of workers who would venture north legally or otherwise to earn a living.[5]

With Kennedy criticizing the bracero program, Congress found it easier to terminate it. Public Law 78, which had been the legal justification for the United States' entrance into a binational labor agreement since 1951, was extended for the final time for one year in December, 1963. In addition, the 1954 binational agreement was extended for the eighth and final time in December 1963.

However, the end of the bracero program in 1964 was Pyrrhic victory for anti-braceroists. This action did not eliminate the Mexican national from the United States' labor scene but encouraged a continuation of wetback labor as well as the immigration of Mexicans who were arbitrarily selected by United States Consuls for employment in the United States. There is at present a total absence of either a binational labor program or a conscientiously administered domestic one. Instead, the latest approach to the Mexican labor program is one of drift without any consistently applied policy.

The California situation illustrates the Mexican worker policy of the Nixon administration. A prominent San Diego physician, Dr. Warren Oaks Kessler, and his wife, Karen Kessler, have personally employed wetbacks and have been involved in attempting to legitimize the status of Mexican workers in the United States. Dr. Kessler estimates that there are 200,000 wetbacks in Southern California alone.[6]

There are a variety of conditions in which Mexicans may now seek entrance to the United States. Mexicans may emigrate with a two-day pass which prohibits them from obtaining employment and restricts their whereabouts to a reasonable distance from the international border. Aliens may also be granted a Green Card which entitles them to find employment in the United States; Green cards are difficult to obtain because United States authorities are apprehensive that the Mexican will forego employment and seek welfare relief from the state. The result is that the worker must post bond to ensure his financial solvency and defray any welfare grants which might subsequently accrue. These bonds are set without any guidelines by United States Consuls in Mexico at between 1,000 and 3,000 dollars. Most alien Mexican workers cannot raise this amount, which accounts for the proliferation of bond companies whose bail bondsmen pay the bonds to the United States Government and in turn exact high interest rates from the Mexicans.

Cenorina was a wetback employed as a domestic as other thousands of Mexican women. Fearful of being deported and unable to protect herself from potential employer abuse, she attempted unsuccessfully for many months to obtain a Green Work Card from the United States Consul in Tijuana, Mexico. She desired legalization, for she often visited her family and was afraid that eventually she would be apprehended as she illegally crossed the border and thereby be prevented from supporting her family. After waiting in interminably long lines at the Consulate she finally obtained the card which legalized her employment status. Although the authorities are aware of whom each Green Card recipient is working for, there is no pretense at guaranteeing just treatment through periodic inspections or through the reintroduction of internationally guaranteed employment and living conditions as established in the binational labor agreements from 1942 to 1954. Not all Mexicans seek Green Cards. Cenorina's brother is an illegal alien working in a Los Angeles industrial firm who never returns to Mexico and does not worry about being discovered.

In the bureaucratic maze of the American Government the United States Consul is the sole determiner of legalization eligibility. Unfortunately, there is a lack of consistent guidelines; the Consul at Tijuana and the Consul at Mexicali may differ as to what the bond should be. The bond is supposedly determined by both the worker's economic worth and the potential employer's financial condition. Cenorina reported having friends who went to different consuls and intended to pay the lowest bond established.

The final report of the Commission on Migratory Labor recommended that the United States centralize and streamline its alien labor administration into a single body to rationalize and determine policy and organization. Yet, the course of events has represented a deterioration of a well-defined bracero policy and the perpetuation of hungry Mexicans having to seek employment in the United States.

The bracero program was born out of idealism in an attempt to utilize hemispheric solidarity in fighting the Axis powers; but through the decades it has degenerated into an unresolved difficult labor problem. The real victims of this sordid affair have been the laborers themselves. United States labor has suffered from the cheap competitive labor which drove down the wages and forced many domestic laborers to seek employment elsewhere. Mexican workers, who sought employment in the United States to alleviate their economic hardships in Mexico, found employment, but labored under either weakly enforced international guarantees or none at all. The future is not promising. The solutions are a rebuilding of the Mexican economy so that it can absorb millions of agricultural laborers and the emergence of United States legislation and administration concern for treatment of farm labor as a human and not as an economic commodity.

NAFTA?

Footnotes:

1. *New York Times*, January 12, 1954; January 16, 1954.

2. *Congressional Record*, 100:561, 2510, 2571.

3. Richard B. Craig, *The Bracero Program, Interest Groups and Foreign Policy* (Austin: University of Texas Press, 1971), pp. 125-126. In 1952, there were 197,000 legally contracted braceros and 543,538 wetbacks. In 1953, the figures were 201,380 and 875,318 respectively; 1954 figures were 309,033 braceros and 1,075,168 known wetbacks.

4. Lee G. Williams, "Recent Legislation Affecting the Mexican Labor Program", *Employment Security Review* 29 (February 1962), 31.

5. *Ibid.*

6. The following was compiled from a series of phone interviews on November 6 and November 7, 1972, with Dr. Warren Oaks Kessler and his wife, Karen Kessler, and personal discussions on November 23 and November 24, 1972.

BIBLIOGRAPHY

Primary Sources

Manuscripts

U. S. Department of Labor Records (RG 174), National Archives, Washington, D.C.

Michael J. Galvin Papers, Truman Library, Independence, Missouri.

John W. Gibson Papers, Truman Library.

Robert Goodwin Papers, Truman Library.

J. Howard McGrath Papers, Truman Library.

Edward G. Miller Papers, Truman Library.

Philleo Nash Papers, Truman Library.

Richard E. Neustadt Papers, Truman Library.

U. S. Office of Defense Transportation (RG 219), National Archives.

President's Commission on Immigration and Naturalization Records, Truman
    Library.

President's Commission on Migratory Labor Records, Truman Library.

John R. Steelman; Office of War Mobilization and Reconversion Records (copies),
    Truman Library.

David H. Stowe Papers, Truman Library.

Harry S. Truman Papers, Truman Library.

U. S. War Manpower Commission (RG 211), National Archives.

Franklin D. Roosevelt Press Conferences, Microfilm, Truman Library.

Interviews

Dr. Warren Oaks Kessler and Ms. Karen Kessler, November 6, 1972; November 7, 1972;
    November 23, 1972; November 24, 1972.

Government Documents

Documents on American Foreign Relations, 10 (January 1-December 31, 1948).

Jones, Robert C. Mexican War Workers in the United States: The Mexico-United States Manpower Recruiting Program and Its Operation. Washington, D.C.: Pan American Union, 1945.

Rasmussen, Wayne D. A History of the Emergency Farm Labor Supply Program 1943-1947. Agriculture Monograph No. 13. Washington, D.C.; U.S. Department of Agriculture, 1951.

Report of the President's Commission on Immigration and Naturalization. Whom We Shall Welcome. Washington, D.C.: Government Printing Office, 1953.

Report of the President's Commission on Migratory Labor. Migratory Labor in American Agriculture. Washington, D.C.: Government Printing Office, 1951.

U. S., Congressional Record. 1942-1964.

U. S. Department of Labor. Labor Press Service, June 12, 1950; July 24, 1950; October, 1951.

U. S. Department of State. "Temporary Migration of Mexican Agricultural Workers, Agreement Between the United States of America and Mexico, Effected by Exchange of Notes Signed August 4, 1942", Executive Agreement Series 278, pp. 1-13. Washington, D.C.; Government Printing Office, 1943.

U. S., Department of State. "Temporary Migration of Mexican Agricultural Workers, Agreement Between the United States of America and Mexico Revising the Agreement of August 4, 1942, Effected by Exchange of Notes Signed at Mexico City April 26, 1943", Executive Agreement Series 351, pp. 1-13. Washington, D.C.; Government Printing Office, 1944.

U. S., Department of State. "Mexican Agricultural Workers, Agreement between the United States of America and Mexico, Effected by Exchange of Notes Signed at Mexico August 1, 1949; Entered into force August 1, 1949 and Amendments and Interpretations, Effected by Exchanges of Notes." TIAS 2260, Treaties and Other International Acts, pp. 1-107, Washington, D.C.; Government Printing Office, 1952.

U. S., Federal Register, 8 (June 23, 1943): 8592-94.

U. S., Statutes at Large, Vols. 56, 57, 58, 59, 60, 61 and 62.

Secondary Sources

Books

Cline, Howard F. The United States and Mexico. Rev. ed. New York: Atheneum, 1968.

Commager, Henry Steele. Documents of American History. New York: Appleton-Century Crofts, 1967.

Craig, Richard B. The Bracero Program: Interest Groups and Foreign Policy. Austin: University of Texas Press, 1971.

Galarza, Ernesto. Merchants of Labor: The Mexican Bracero Story. Charlotte: McNally and Loftin, 1967.

Grebler, Leo; Moore, Joan W.; and Guzman, Ralph C. The Mexican American People: The Nation's Second Largest Minority. New York: The Free Press, 1970.

Hughes, Everett C., and Hughes, Helen MacGill. Where People Meet: Racial and Ethnic Frontiers. New York: The Free Press, 1952.

Lamb, Ruth S. Mexican Americans: Sons of the Southwest. Claremont: Ocelot Press, 1970.

Matusow, Allen J. Farm Policies and Politics in the Truman Years. Cambridge: Harvard University Press, 1967.

McConnell, Grant. The Decline of Agrarian Democracy. Berkeley: University of California Press, 1953.

McGovern, George S., ed. Agricultural Thought in the Twentieth Century. Indianapolis: Bobbs-Merrill, 1967.

McWilliams, Carey. North from Mexico. New York: Greenwood Press, 1968.

Moquin, Wayne. A Documentary History of the Mexican American. New York: Praeger, 1971.

Nava, Julian. Mexican Americans: A Brief Look at Their History. New York: Anti-Defamation League of B'nai B'rith, 1970.

Servin, Manuel P. The Mexican Americans: An Awakening Majority. Beverly Hills: Glencoe Press, 1970.

Simpson, Lesley Byrd. Many Mexicos. 4th ed. Berkeley: University of California Press, 1967.

Articles

"Across the Border", Business Week, July 31, 1943, pp. 85-86.

Almazán, Marco A. "The Mexicans Keep 'Em Rolling", The Inter-American, 4 (October 1945): 20-23, 36.

Álvarez, José Hernandez. "A Demographic Profile of the Mexican Immigration to the United States, 1910-1950", Journal of Inter-American Studies, 8 (July 1966): 471-496.

"Back to the Homeland", The Survey, 69 (January 1933): 39.

Begeman, Jean. "Sweatshops on the Farm". New Republic, July 30, 1951, pp. 16-17.

"Braceros". Fortune, 43 (April 1951): 58-65.

Cardenas, Reymundo, "The Mexican in Adrian". Michigan History, 42 (September 1958): 343-52.

Coalson, George O. "Mexican Contract Labor in American Agriculture". Southwestern Social Science Quarterly, 33 (December 1952): 228-238.

Crawford, Remsen. "The Menace of Mexican Immigration". Current History, 31 (February 1930): 902-07.

"Did They Attack the Root?" Commonweal, April 20, 1951, p. 29.

"Drying Wetbacks". Business Week, July 21, 1951, p. 127.

"The Farm Labor Fiasco". Nation, August 18, 1951, p. 124.

Galindo, Antonio Ruiz. "Economic Situation of Mexico in 1947". The Social Sciences in Mexico and South and Central America, 1 (Winter 1947-48): 1-6.

Gilmore, N. Ray, and Gladys W. Gilmore. "The Bracero in California". Pacific Historical Review, 32 (August 1963): 265-282.

Goott, Daniel. "Employment of Foreign Workers in United States Agriculture". Department of State Bulletin, July 18, 1949, pp. 43-46.

Hawley, Ellis W. "The Politics of the Mexican Labor Issue, 1950-1965". Agricultural History, 40 (July 1966): 157-176.

"Imported Hands". Business Week, May 29, 1943, pp. 23-24.

Issler, Anne Roller. "Good Neighbors Lend a Hand: Our Mexican Workers". Survey Graphic, 32 (October 1943): 389-394

Korcik, William. "The Wetback Story". Commonweal, July 13, 1951, pp. 327-29.

"Letters to the Editor". The Inter-American, 3 (November 1944): 47-48.

Lopez Malo, Ernesto. "La Emigracion de Trabajadores Mexicanos". Ciencias Sociales, 5 (October 1954): 220-27.

McWilliams, Carey. "They Saved the Crops". The Inter-American, 2 (August 1943): 10-14.

"Mexican-American Commission for Economic Cooperation". Bulletin of the Pan American Union. 79 (April 1945): 211-15.

"Mexican Exodus". Newsweek, July 31, 1939, p. 11.

"Mexican View of Race Relations". The Inter-American, 2 (September 1943): 38.

"Mexicans Assist". Business Week, October 14, 1944, p. 54.

"Mexicans Mitigate Labor Scarcity". Railway Age, June 10, 1944, pp. 1112-16.

"Migrant Labor Agreement with Mexico". Department of State Bulletin, August 27, 1951, p. 336.

Motley, Arthur W. "Mexico Helps War Effort of Our Railroads". Manpower Review, December 1943, pp. 10-11.

"Murder on the Rio Grande". Newsweek, October 8, 1945, p. 71.

"Negotiations for New Agreement on Importing Mexican Workers to U.S." Department of State Bulletin, July 30, 1951, p. 199.

"No Mexicans Allowed". The Inter-American, 2 (September 1943): 8-9.

"Nonimmigrant Passport Visa Fee Agreements with Mexico". Department of State Bulletin, May 29, 1950, pp. 870-73.

Parks, Marion. "A New Pattern in International Wartime Collaboration". Department of State Bulletin, August 13, 1944, pp. 160-65.

"Railroads' Burden". Business Week, January 1, 1944, pp. 44-46.

"Relief". The Survey, 73 (March 1937): 82-83.

Rippy, J. Fred. "Border Troubles Along the Rio Grande". Southwestern Historical Quarterly, 23 (October 1919): 91-111.

"Rules for Admission of Mexican Workers as Railroad Track Laborers". Monthly Labor Review, August 1943, pp. 240-41.

Scruggs, Otey M. "The Bracero Program Under the Farm Security Administration, 1942-1943". Labor History, 3 (Spring, 1962): 149-68.

_____. "Evolution of the Mexican Farm Labor Agreement of 1942". Agricultural History, 34 (July 1960): 140-49.

_____. "Texas and the Bracero Program". Pacific Historical Review, 32 (February 1963); 251-64.

"A Touchy Subject". The Inter-American, 3 (August 1944): 32.

"U. S. and Mexico Reach Agreement on Agricultural Workers". Department of State Bulletin, February 19, 1951, p. 300.

"U. S., Mexico to Extend Migratory Labor Agreement". Department of State Bulletin, March 3, 1952, p. 359.

"U. S., Mexico Extend Migratory Labor Agreement". Department of State Bulletin, June 23, 1952, p. 985.

"Wetbacks". Newsweek, March 11, 1946, pp. 70-71.

Woodbridge, Hensley C. "Mexico and U. S. Racism: How Mexicans View Our Treatment of Minorities". Commonweal, June 22, 1945, pp. 234-37.

Newspapers

Accion, October 22, 1951

Excelsior (Mexico City), July 20, 1951; September 13, 1951.

El Heraldo, October 2, 1951.

El Informador (Guadalajara), September 15, 1951.

New York Times, 1934-1953.

El Norte (Monterrey), October 2, 1951; October 3, 1951.

El Occidental (Chihuahua), October 18, 1951.

El Paso Times. August 9, 1952.

Pecos Enterprise, August 11, 1952.

La Prensa, September 17, 1951.

The Reporter, August 6, 1952.

San Angelo Standard Times, August 2, 1951; August 3, 1952.

El Sol del Centro, September 16, 1951.

Washington Post, 1951-1952.